New Dayl

C000230360

Edited by **Gordon Giles**   January–April 2023

15 The Chambers, Vineyard
Abingdon OX14 3FE
brf.org.uk

Bible Reading Fellowship is a charity (233280) and company
limited by guarantee (301324), registered in England and Wales

ISBN 978 1 80039 190 1
All rights reserved

This edition © Bible Reading Fellowship 2022
Cover image: Mill Lane, Halnaker, West Sussex © Lois GoBe/stock.adobe.com;
p. 143: iPad drawing © Martin Beek

Distributed in Australia by:
MediaCom Education Inc, PO Box 610, Unley, SA 5061
Tel: 1 800 811 311 | admin@mediacom.org.au

Distributed in New Zealand by:
Scripture Union Wholesale, PO Box 760, Wellington 6140
Tel: 04 385 0421 | suwholesale@clear.net.nz

Acknowledgements

Scripture quotations marked with the following abbreviations are taken from the
version shown. **NIV:** The Holy Bible, New International Version, Anglicised edition,
copyright © 1979, 1984, 2011 by Biblica. Used by permission of Hodder & Stoughton
Publishers, an Hachette UK company. All rights reserved. 'NIV' is a registered
trademark of Biblica. UK trademark number 1448790. **NRSV:** The New Revised
Standard Version of the Bible, Anglicised Edition, copyright © 1989, 1995 by the
Division of Christian Education of the National Council of the Churches of Christ
in the USA. Used by permission. All rights reserved. **GNT:** The Good News Bible
published by The Bible Societies/HarperCollins Publishers Ltd, UK © American
Bible Society 1966, 1971, 1976, 1992, used with permission.

A catalogue record for this book is available from the British Library

Printed by Gutenberg Press, Tarxien, Malta

Suggestions for using *New Daylight*

Find a regular time and place, if possible, where you can read and pray undisturbed. Before you begin, take time to be still and perhaps use the BRF prayer on page 6. Then read the Bible passage slowly (try reading it aloud if you find it over-familiar), followed by the comment. You can also use *New Daylight* for group study and discussion, if you prefer.

The prayer or point for reflection can be a starting point for your own meditation and prayer. Many people like to keep a journal to record their thoughts about a Bible passage and items for prayer. In *New Daylight* we also note the Sundays and some special festivals from the church calendar, to keep in step with the Christian year.

New Daylight and the Bible

New Daylight contributors use a range of Bible versions, and you will find a list of the versions used opposite. You are welcome to use your own preferred version alongside the passage printed in the notes. This can be particularly helpful if the Bible text has been abridged.

New Daylight affirms that the whole of the Bible is God's revelation to us, and we should read, reflect on and learn from every part of both Old and New Testaments. Usually the printed comment presents a straightforward 'thought for the day', but sometimes it may also raise questions rather than simply providing answers, as we wrestle with some of the more difficult passages of scripture.

New Daylight is also available in a compact size edition. Visit your local Christian bookshop or BRF's online shop **brfonline.org.uk**. To obtain a cassette version for the visually impaired, contact Torch Trust for the Blind, Torch House, Torch Way, Northampton Road, Market Harborough LE16 9HL; +44 (0)1858 438260; **info@torchtrust.org**. For a Braille edition, contact St John's Guild, Sovereign House, 12–14 Warwick Street, Coventry CV5 6ET; +44 (0)24 7671 4241; **info@stjohnsguild.org**.

Comment on *New Daylight*

To send feedback, please email **enquiries@brf.org.uk**, phone **+44 (0)1865 319700** or write to the address shown opposite.

Writers in this issue

Amy Boucher Pye is an author, speaker and spiritual director. She's a regular contributor to several devotional publications and her books include *7 Ways to Pray*, *The Living Cross* and *Celebrating Christmas*.

Paul Gravelle is an Anglican priest in Auckland, New Zealand. He is a poet, writer and retreat leader and has ministered in military, urban and rural settings, supporting himself as an industrial journalist.

Terry Hinks is a United Reformed Church minister, serving two churches in the High Wycombe area. His special interests are Christian unity, community engagement and the care of God's creation, alongside a deep love of the Bible, stillness and prayer.

Liz Hoare is an ordained Anglican priest and teaches spiritual formation at Wycliffe Hall, Oxford. Her interests lie in the history and literature of Christian spirituality and their connections with the today's world.

Andy John is the archbishop of Wales and bishop of Bangor, where he has served for more than a decade. Andy is a Kiwi (his mother's side) and Welsh cross (his father's side) and has spent all his ministry in the Church in Wales. Apart from being a bishop he occasionally attempts marathons.

Ann Lewin taught RE and English for 27 years, then spent the last years of her working life as a welfare adviser to international university students. She has had a great deal of experience of leading retreats and quiet days.

Margaret Silf is an ecumenical Christian committed to working across and beyond traditional divisions. She is the author of a number of books for 21st-century spiritual pilgrims and a retreat facilitator. She is a mother and grandmother and lives in North Staffordshire.

Amy Scott Robinson is the author of several books, including *Images of Grace* (BRF, 2022). After studying English at Christ's College, Cambridge, she trained as a teacher and co-founded a business for storytelling in education. Amy is a regular contributor to the *Church Times*.

David Walker is the bishop of Manchester and chair of the board of Church Commissioners. He is a regular broadcaster on BBC radio, including the *Daily Service* and *Sunday*. He is also the author of two BRF books: *God's Belongers* (2017) and *You Are Mine* (2019).

Gordon Giles writes...

 Happy New Year! Some people have started calling the gap between Christmas and New Year 'Twixmas'. This is not a reference to the chocolate bar, but is instead based on the archaic word 'betwixt'. The days between (betwixt) Christmas and New Year are the in-between days, dominated by shopping, relaxation, entertainment, sport and family time. When it's over, it is New Year, and another date, another calendar, another year and another edition of *New Daylight* begins.

In 1931 Walter de la Mare published a book of children's poetry entitled *Tom Tiddler's Ground*, in which he included a poem that three years later the composer Benjamin Britten set to music as 'A New Year Carol'. The title is the name of a children's game referred to by Charles Dickens in a short story of the same name written in 1861 and in various of his novels. The carol begins: 'Here we bring new water from the well so clear, for to worship God with, this happy New Year.' Successive verses contain the lines: 'Open you the west door and turn the old year go' and 'Open you the east door and let the New Year in'.

Children's games aside, this little masterpiece is set in church, with the east and west doors at each respective end, first opened at the west end, to let the old year depart in peace, and then at the east end, where resides the high altar, the holy end, if you like, to welcome in the New Year. The font is at the west end, full of water, and the altar at the east, where we are reminded of Holy Communion, where the blood of Christ is wine. The carol's refrain, 'Levy-dew, sing levy-due, the water and the wine', brings these together, briefly and sweetly.

As we open the east door, having ushered out the old to the setting sunset in the west, we bring in the dawn of 2023, praying and hoping that it may be a good year, not only for the newborns and those who are older, but for everyone betwixt. We pray for you, gentle readers, that daily fed by God's word, you may continue to be grounded in faith, inspired in hope and led by God's love.

Welcome! Welcome to a new year.

REVD CANON DR GORDON GILES

The BRF Prayer

Faithful God,
thank you for growing BRF
from small beginnings
into a worldwide family of ministries.
We rejoice as young and old
discover you through your word
and grow daily in faith and love.
Keep us humble in your service,
ambitious for your glory
and open to new opportunities.
For your name's sake,
Amen

Helping to pay it forward

As part of our Living Faith ministry, we're raising funds to give away copies of Bible reading notes and other resources to those who aren't able to access them any other way, working with foodbanks and chaplaincy services, in prisons, hospitals and care homes.

If you've enjoyed and benefited from our resources, would you consider paying it forward to enable others to do so too?

Make a gift at **brf.org.uk/donate**

The Word made flesh: John 1—2

What better place to begin the new year, and this eighth day of Christmas, than with John's gospel? John had a high view of Jesus as the Messiah, the Christ, God who took human form in a baby, which we're celebrating during this Christmas season.

John's gospel differs from those of the other, 'synoptic' gospels – Matthew, Mark and Luke – in a few key ways, one of which is how he starts the story. Instead of recounting the birth narrative or looking at Jesus' genealogy, John goes back to the beginning, to Jesus being with God at the foundation of the world. The opening of John's gospel reveals how he is concerned not only with the nature of God in the form of the Trinity – God the Father, Son and Holy Spirit – but also, albeit only hinted at, with the mystical union that followers of Jesus have with God, one of John's major themes.

In his gospel, John shares the revelation that Jesus is the Saviour, the Messiah, and that true worship can only exist in and through him. As we see in the prologue, Jesus was there with God in the beginning and indeed was God; he then became flesh and set up camp among us. After this amazing opening, John shares how Jesus is the Messiah through seven miracles, and then gives us a unique insight into Jesus' last days before his death and resurrection. John's recounting of Jesus' last discussion with his friends after their final supper is filled with special promises about life after he dies.

This week we are journeying with John through his first two chapters. After exploring the prologue, we will engage with the gently invitational way Jesus gathers his disciples. Then we encounter his first miracle, when he rescues a wedding party in danger of social collapse when the wine is running out, and finally we shall look at the episode when Jesus clears out the temple. John places this incident at the beginning of his three-year public ministry, in contrast to the synoptic gospels, which time it during the last week of his life.

I pray that, as you begin 2023, you will know the loving and transforming presence of Jesus through the Spirit, leading you to the Father.

AMY BOUCHER PYE

The Word

In the beginning was the Word, and the Word was with God, and the Word was God. He was with God in the beginning. Through him all things were made; without him nothing was made that has been made. In him was life, and that life was the light of all mankind. The light shines in the darkness, and the darkness has not overcome it… He came to that which was his own, but his own did not receive him. Yet to all who did receive him, to those who believed in his name, he gave the right to become children of God… The Word became flesh and made his dwelling among us. We have seen his glory, the glory of the one and only Son, who came from the Father, full of grace and truth.

John's prologue packs in so much goodness and truth in 18 verses; note what he communicates even in the first line. He hearkens back to Genesis by using the same opening as the one there and by employing some of the words found in the creation account: life, light, darkness. He then reveals some of the mystery of Jesus and the Father: the Word was – Jesus existed with God before the creation of time; the Word was with God – he lived in community with God; and the Word was God – their union exceeds our understanding.

Not only is Jesus God, but he became man and dwelt among us (v. 14). The word for 'dwelling' means to live in a tent, and the original readers would have known the Old Testament reference to God dwelling in the tabernacle in the wilderness. This same verb appears in Revelation in two places, including the lovely line, 'Look! God's dwelling-place is now among the people, and he will dwell with them' (Revelation 21:3).

Why not spend time pondering some of the mystery and wonder of John's prologue? You could read through the passage several times, asking God to highlight a word or phrase as you do, chewing over it and responding to the triune God.

Loving God, your love for us knows no bounds. Fill me with gratitude and awe for the gift of life and light, which I receive through Jesus. Amen

AMY BOUCHER PYE

True humility

Now this was John's testimony when the Jewish leaders in Jerusalem sent priests and Levites to ask him who he was. He did not fail to confess, but confessed freely, 'I am not the Messiah.' They asked him, 'Then who are you? Are you Elijah?' He said, 'I am not.' 'Are you the Prophet?' He answered, 'No.' Finally they said, 'Who are you? Give us an answer to take back to those who sent us. What do you say about yourself?' John replied in the words of Isaiah the prophet, 'I am the voice of one calling in the wilderness, "Make straight the way for the Lord."'

John the Baptist knows who he is, and he is not about to puff himself up. When interrogated by the religious leaders who wonder why he attracts so many crowds, he replies with one-word answers. When pushed to say who he is, he responds that he is a voice, in contrast to Jesus being the Word, as we saw yesterday. John is simply a voice heralding the real deal.

How refreshing is this humility! In contrast, we can probably call to mind more than one person who makes outlandish comments about themselves, usually rooted in pride or insecurity. More often than not, the truth will come out and they will be shown for who they really are.

Instead, true humility grasps an understanding of who God is and who we are in relation to him, which John the Baptist knew. Although he stayed true to his commission of being the voice in the wilderness, he also acknowledged that he was not worthy to untie the straps of the one coming after him (John 1:27).

As you think about John the Baptist, consider how you reconcile being God's child and made in his image with a healthy dose of humility, and how you work that out in daily life. Consider too if you might need to make any adjustments, either in terms of embracing more humility or standing strong in your identity.

'Take my yoke upon you and learn from me, for I am gentle and humble in heart, and you will find rest for your souls' (Matthew 11:29).

AMY BOUCHER PYE

Jesus and the Spirit

The next day John saw Jesus coming towards him and said, 'Look, the Lamb of God, who takes away the sin of the world!... I myself did not know him, but the reason I came baptising with water was that he might be revealed to Israel.' Then John gave this testimony: 'I saw the Spirit come down from heaven as a dove and remain on him. And I myself did not know him, but the one who sent me to baptise with water told me, "The man on whom you see the Spirit come down and remain is the one who will baptise with the Holy Spirit." I have seen and I testify that this is God's Chosen One.'

As this passage may be familiar to you, I invite you to ponder two fascinating parts of it. One concerns how it reflects aspects of the Trinity – the Father, Son and Holy Spirit. They are one and they dwell in each other and yet are unique persons. We will never fully fathom this mystery, but we can still delight in reflecting upon it.

As you consider the Trinity, note that John the Baptist sees the Spirit descend on Jesus. My thought is, surely that's not the first time the Spirit alighted on Jesus, as they were together before the foundation of the world, right? Extending this line of thinking to those who are baptised, is baptism the first time the Spirit rests on us? Perhaps sometimes our physical baptism comes after a spiritual baptism. These are interesting questions to chew on.

Another aspect to ponder is the word 'remain'. John sees the Spirit 'remain' on Jesus, and this alerts him to the divine revelation that Jesus is 'God's Chosen One' (John 1:34). Much later, in the week before he dies, Jesus urges his friends to 'remain' in him so that they can produce fruit (see John 15:4). We remain in Jesus, and he remains in us through the work of the Holy Spirit. What an amazing and life-giving mystery!

Indwelling Jesus, just as you are in the Father and the Father is in you, so you welcome me to remain in you. Help me to do so by the power of your Spirit, that I might bear lasting fruit. Amen

AMY BOUCHER PYE

Come and see

The next day John was there again with two of his disciples. When he saw Jesus passing by, he said, 'Look, the Lamb of God!' When the two disciples heard him say this, they followed Jesus. Turning round, Jesus saw them following and asked, 'What do you want?' They said, 'Rabbi' (which means 'Teacher'), 'where are you staying?' 'Come,' he replied, 'and you will see.' So they went and saw where he was staying, and they spent that day with him… The first thing Andrew did was to find his brother Simon and tell him, 'We have found the Messiah' (that is, the Christ). And he brought him to Jesus. Jesus looked at him and said, 'You are Simon son of John. You will be called Cephas' (which, when translated, is Peter).

When John the Baptist testifies that Jesus is the sacrificial Lamb of God, his disciples – Andrew and probably John, the gospel writer – start following Jesus. They understand that he is the Messiah, the Christ, and they do not want to keep this secret to themselves. For instance, Andrew immediately searches out his brother and therefore makes a key introduction in the life of the church. This is Simon, whom Jesus says will become Peter, which means 'rock'.

We know that later Jesus reaffirms his identity and promises, 'I tell you that you are Peter, and on this rock I will build my church, and the gates of Hades will not overcome it' (Matthew 16:18). Perhaps no one was more surprised by this declaration than Simon, for as we see in the gospel accounts, he was often impulsive and hasty. But God transformed him.

When Jesus speaks to his new friends, notice how invitational he is. He asks them what they want and then welcomes them to journey with him. Come, he says, and experience for yourself.

We too can extend this gentle invitation for people to come and see. And we, like Andrew, can share our enthusiasm about finding the Saviour, the one who meets us and lovingly changes us. Just as Jesus did with Simon becoming the rock upon which the church was built.

Loving God, you welcome us to come just as we are into your presence. Meet me, change me and transform me more into the person you created me to be. Amen

AMY BOUCHER PYE

'Follow me'

Finding Philip, [Jesus] said to him, 'Follow me'... Philip found Nathanael and told him, 'We have found the one Moses wrote about in the Law, and about whom the prophets also wrote – Jesus of Nazareth, the son of Joseph.' 'Nazareth! Can anything good come from there?' Nathanael asked. 'Come and see,' said Philip. When Jesus saw Nathanael approaching, he said of him, 'Here truly is an Israelite in whom there is no deceit.' 'How do you know me?' Nathanael asked. Jesus answered, 'I saw you while you were still under the fig-tree before Philip called you.' Then Nathanael declared, 'Rabbi, you are the Son of God; you are the king of Israel.' Jesus said, 'You believe because I told you I saw you under the fig-tree. You will see greater things than that.'

We might be surprised to realise that although Jesus called Philip directly to follow him, he did not single out any of the others. Not even those we consider to be in the 'inner circle' – John and Peter. Rather, Jesus called an ordinary man, Philip, to leave what he was doing and to follow him.

Philip consented and soon realised that this was what they had been waiting for: the one Moses wrote about. Then Jesus used extraordinary means to reveal to Nathanael his identity. Although Nathanael was blown away, Jesus says that is not all – he will see much more if he sticks with him.

Note therefore the different ways that Jesus' disciples came to him. Often, they heard about him from someone they knew and trusted; more rarely, he sought them out directly; and sometimes, he used a revelation to confirm his identity. But whatever the route, Jesus never coerced his followers nor tried to bend their wills to his. Rather, he extended a gracious invitation to come, taste, follow and live. One that he continues to make today, most usually through his ambassadors, those whom like Andrew and Philip extend his invitation to come and see.

Lord Jesus, you fulfilled the prophecies of old. Open my eyes to see, open my ears to hear and open my heart to receive the wonders you bestow on those who love and serve you. Amen

AMY BOUCHER PYE

The best for now

When the wine was gone, Jesus' mother said to him, 'They have no more wine.' 'Woman, why do you involve me?' Jesus replied. 'My hour has not yet come.' His mother said to the servants, 'Do whatever he tells you.' … Jesus said to the servants, 'Fill the jars with water'; so they filled them to the brim. Then he told them, 'Now draw some out and take it to the master of the banquet.' They did so, and the master of the banquet tasted the water that had been turned into wine… He called the bridegroom aside and said, 'Everyone brings out the choice wine first and then the cheaper wine after the guests have had too much to drink; but you have saved the best till now.'

After detailing the calling of Jesus' disciples, John begins to explore Jesus' public ministry, starting with the first of seven miracles or, as John calls them, signs. Two things stand out as I read this familiar story again.

The first is how Jesus signals to his mother that their relationship has changed, namely through calling her 'Woman'. If she is hurt by this, she does not show it; instead she affirms her belief in Jesus by telling the servants to follow his lead. As we ponder Mary's change in status, we can consider if Jesus is calling us to relate to him differently, even if that feels painful at first.

The second thing that stands out is the simplicity and earthiness of Jesus' first miracle. Jesus could have created an almighty display of wonder and power, but instead he involved the servants in a simple act of turning water into wine. He did not declare what he had done to those who were seen as important – the master of the banquet – but quietly produced a miracle. We might ask ourselves how often we look for mighty displays when God instead meets our needs in more humble ways. And are we willing to obey him, as the servants did?

Jesus, you enjoyed a party and did not want the hosts to be embarrassed. Help me to embrace a sense of abundance when it comes to understanding who you are and how much you love me. Amen

AMY BOUCHER PYE

A clean temple

In the temple courts [Jesus] found people selling cattle, sheep and doves, and others sitting at tables exchanging money. So he made a whip out of cords, and drove all from the temple courts... 'Stop turning my Father's house into a market!' His disciples remembered that it is written: 'Zeal for your house will consume me.' The Jews then responded to him, 'What sign can you show us to prove your authority to do all this?' Jesus answered them, 'Destroy this temple, and I will raise it again in three days.' They replied, 'It has taken forty-six years to build this temple, and you are going to raise it in three days?' But the temple he had spoken of was his body.

This first public appearance of Jesus follows his calling of the disciples and the first miracle at Cana. Through it he reveals the need for purity in worship and the price he will pay in providing the means for people to be united with his Father by his death and resurrection. At the wedding he performed a sign revealing his divine nature, and in the cleansing of the temple he revealed a promise that they did not yet understand: that through his death and rising again, they would no longer even need a temple.

The temple had been the place for God's presence to dwell, but Jesus would reveal a different way. He later promised his disciples that he would send the Holy Spirit to be with them and to live in them (see John 14—17). Thus God would be present within his followers dotted around the world. And if we are the temple of the Holy Spirit, Jesus must desire that we keep ourselves clean, just as he zealously cleared the temple of that which was polluting it.

This week we have seen how the Word was God and dwelled among us; that he called his disciples; how he gave generously and miraculously of himself; and how Jesus guarded the purity of God's house zealously. What will you take away from this time in John's gospel?

Gracious God, set into place all that you would have me glean
from the riches of your word. Amen

AMY BOUCHER PYE

Jude the Obscure

It is not often within the pages of these notes that we read a biblical book in its entirety. With this letter we can put our scissors away and read the complete published works of St Jude.

His is perhaps an unfamiliar voice, and his words are rarely heard. The whole letter is read once a year in the Church of England, at a weekday evening prayer in the last week of Advent. An extract from his letter is also read on 29 October each year, the day on which Jude is celebrated, sharing the honours with St Simon (the zealot).

Having the same or a very similar name to the infamous Judas Iscariot has clouded Jude's fame, and for that reason he was rarely relied on as a saint for intercession in the medieval church. Instead, he gained a reputation as a last resort for prayer and became known as the patron saint of lost causes.

Jude's letter does not tell us much about himself, other than that he was a 'servant of Christ and brother of James'. In Luke 6:16 Jude, or Judas, is described as the 'son' of James, but it also seems he is the same person as Thaddaeus (Matthew 10:3). His brother James is referred to as brother of the Lord (Galatians 1:19) and, according to Paul, was one of the first to see the risen Christ (1 Corinthians 15:7). In Mark's gospel the family picture is more in focus, as it is asked of Jesus: 'Is not this the carpenter, the son of Mary and brother of James and Joses and Judas and Simon, and are not his sisters here with us?' (Mark 6:3, NRSV; also see Matthew 13:55).

So Jude is well-connected. Even if, as in verse 17 of his letter, he does distance himself from the disciples, he effectively presents himself as a brother of Jesus. His disinclination to say this outright is often attributed to humility, by none other than Clement of Alexandria (died c. AD215). Another point to note is that if Jude was born around AD10 (being much younger than Jesus) and the letter was written around AD80, then Jude would have been about 70 years old when he wrote the letter.

There is little reason to doubt that Jude, a Jew, a brother of Jesus and an apostle, wrote this letter. So let us begin to see how and why.

GORDON GILES

Driven to distraction

Jude, a servant of Jesus Christ and brother of James, to those who are called, who are beloved in God the Father and kept safe for Jesus Christ: May mercy, peace, and love be yours in abundance. Beloved, while eagerly preparing to write to you about the salvation we share, I find it necessary to write and appeal to you to contend for the faith that was once for all entrusted to the saints. For certain intruders have stolen in among you, people who long ago were designated for this condemnation as ungodly, who pervert the grace of our God into licentiousness and deny our only Master and Lord, Jesus Christ.

Do you ever get distracted? It is so easy to be derailed from whatever activity we are, or are supposed to be, engaged in, by other matters. It is not the same as procrastination: avoiding tasks that need to be done by engaging in deflection activities. We might put off doing the cleaning by finding all sorts of 'more important' tasks, which we push to the top of our to-do list in order to avoid it!

This is not what has happened to Jude. He is driven to distraction on hearing that 'intruders have stolen in among' them, leading them astray from the gospel of Christ. These are travelling teachers who have twisted Christian teaching in such a way as to permit attitudes and behaviour which contradict the purity and faith which Jude himself would have remembered Jesus teaching. This means that instead of writing them a leisurely letter of friendly greeting and affirmative fellowship, as he had planned to, Jude feels forced to address the fact that they are being led astray.

Jude could have been writing to every church ever since. His opening lines demonstrate his love for them – he is a true pastor – but also reveal how the ways of the world can intrude and distract. The history of the church is of erring and straying, or being led by popular or contemporary trends, and ultimately of discerning if and how new thinking is compatible with authentic gospel values.

What do you think? Is the church you love struggling with distraction at this time? What is the loving, authentic response?

Father God, help me focus on you, always. Amen

GORDON GILES

You should know better

Now I desire to remind you, though you are fully informed, that the Lord, who once for all saved a people out of the land of Egypt, afterwards destroyed those who did not believe. And the angels who did not keep their own position, but left their proper dwelling, he has kept in eternal chains in deepest darkness for the judgement of the great day. Likewise, Sodom and Gomorrah and the surrounding cities, which, in the same manner as they, indulged in sexual immorality and pursued unnatural lust, serve as an example by undergoing a punishment of eternal fire.

Parents say to their children, 'You should know better', and adults use the phrase to remind others that they have made an avoidable moral mistake for which they must take responsibility. It is a way of saying, 'It's your own fault. Do not try to blame anyone else or say that you were unaware of what you were doing.' From childish errors to concentration camp guards, ignorance is no excuse when one can be expected to know the action is wrong. Yet human beings have frequently and consistently let themselves down in every context and age, to varying degrees of severity.

Jude's readers are living amid a permissive and pagan society. One of the strengths of his pastoral approach is that, while he rebukes, he is also loving. Jude cares for his readers, yet still tells them off, not high-handedly, but more in the spirit of 'You have let yourselves down and are better than that.' It is the manner many adopt to help young people learn better behaviour for themselves, rather than simply be punished or lectured.

Yet there are still consequences of which to be reminded; his readers will know of those who disbelieved (Israel), disobeyed (fallen angels) and sinned (Sodom and Gomorrah). Although not always biblical, Jude refers to traditions in which his readers were well-versed, including the story of how angels succumbed to pride and so fell from grace (found in 1 Enoch, an ancient Jewish text deemed by most Christians and Jews to be inauthentic scripture). Even today we remind ourselves of these things as we know that in Christ, love and judgement go together, in this and every age.

Lord Jesus, help me to follow you and not be led astray. Amen

GORDON GILES

Irreverent arrogance

Yet in the same way these dreamers also defile the flesh, reject author-ity, and slander the glorious ones. But when the archangel Michael contended with the devil and disputed about the body of Moses, he did not dare to bring a condemnation of slander against him, but said, 'The Lord rebuke you!' But these people slander whatever they do not understand, and they are destroyed by those things that, like irrational animals, they know by instinct.

Have you met people who make up their own version of faith, attributing it to Christianity and then resisting any challenge or criticism? When wear-ing my clerical collar, I sometimes meet people in the street or at social gatherings who tell me their version of faith. They think that, as a Christian minister, first, I am interested to hear their version of religion and, second, I will agree with it, because, after all, we all make up our own minds about life and faith, don't we?

Seriously, though, it is a modern attitude with ancient precursors, which emboldens people who have barely read the Bible to appropriate, adapt and advocate a belief system of their own concoction, even if it either leaves out so much of Christian teaching, or borrows from other philosophies to such an extent, as to be virtually unrecognisable as Christian. We used to call such things 'heresy'. Perhaps we still should. That Christian living has to a great extent been stripped of its purity comes as no surprise nowadays. What may be a surprise is that this is not new.

Jude condemns those who dream up new versions of faith as lustful, irreverent rebels. In arrogance they reject God's authority, exult in their own knowledge and dismiss the supernatural. Rather they might remember mythical stories about Michael being careful how he engaged with Satan when Moses died, and be wary as mortals how they speak and behave mor-ally and spiritually. Ultimately everything is in the hands and judgement of God, and it is dangerous to go by instinct or make it up as you go along. Rather, integrity, humility and spiritual sensitivity are needed.

Guide me, my great redeemer and lead me in your paths alone. Amen

GORDON GILES

Feast on love

Woe to them! For they go the way of Cain, and abandon themselves to Balaam's error for the sake of gain, and perish in Korah's rebellion. These are blemishes on your love-feasts, while they feast with you without fear, feeding themselves. They are waterless clouds carried along by the winds; autumn trees without fruit, twice dead, uprooted; wild waves of the sea, casting up the foam of their own shame; wandering stars, for whom the deepest darkness has been reserved forever.

The Covid-19 pandemic brought out the best and the worst in people. We saw deep caring for others at the hands of the NHS and volunteers looking out for the isolated, sick or suffering. We saw generosity as some funded vaccines and those who were in financial need. But we also saw greed and corruption as the crisis was exploited by some for monetary gain. Some people made a lot of money out of Covid. We have also seen leadership operate in extremity, gaining support, but also provoking resistance, resentment and even rebellion.

Notice that the three characters whom Jude criticises here are Cain, who cared not for anyone else, not even his brother, whom he killed; Balaam, who was greedy and acquisitive; and Korah, who rejected the authority of others' leadership. These three archetypal characters have descendants among us still. In Jude's day the connection is made with those who behave badly at the early celebrations of Holy Communion, rather like the agape or 'bring and share' meals we might have experienced. The Eucharist took place within the context of an ordinary meal, as indeed had the original last supper. The apostle Paul reminds us of this and of those who defiled it by consuming what they brought and not sharing (See 1 Corinthians 11:20–22). For Jude, they are like clouds who promise but do not deliver rain; like fruitless trees; like waves that leave scum on the shore; or stars that have no direction or destination.

Jude's condemnations are harsh but can inspire pity for those who, in any age, are so entrapped by bad behaviour that they miss the liberating, loving alternatives to which Christ calls us.

Jesus, give us love so that in faith we may bring hope to others. Amen

GORDON GILES

Do we ever learn?

It was also about these that Enoch, in the seventh generation from Adam, prophesied, saying, 'See, the Lord is coming with ten thousands of his holy ones, to execute judgement on all, and to convict everyone of all the deeds of ungodliness that they have committed in such an ungodly way, and of all the harsh things that ungodly sinners have spoken against him.' These are grumblers and malcontents; they indulge their own lusts; they are bombastic in speech, flattering people to their own advantage.

Many theologians say that faith in practice is built on 'scripture, reason and tradition', a phrase associated with Joseph Butler and Richard Hooker, whose views helped define Anglicanism, to some extent in reaction to Puritanism. Others prefer *solo scriptura* (scripture alone). Here Jude draws not only on scripture, but also on the traditional stories of Judaism and on what he knows of his personal relationship with Christ. And so he builds a rational argument. His letter is an impressive piece of early theology.

Enoch was a descendant of Adam, through his third son Seth (Genesis 5). The book 1 Enoch is not regarded as scripture by Jews or Christians, but it is part of the tradition known to and respected by Jews of Jude's day, to whom he was writing. Similarly, there are writers (ancient and modern) whom the Christian tradition has come to respect as wise and profound, such as Augustine, Aquinas, Luther and Calvin.

More to the point, Jude is using a passage from tradition to illustrate that there is truth in the prediction that the Lord will come in judgement (which we also find in Matthew 24:29–31) and that these bombastic flatterers who are distracting the true Christians will get their comeuppance. Jude's message here is observe history and learn from tradition.

Do we ever learn? Do we see history repeating itself in our day? It seems there will always be strife and war, and the church is 'by schisms rent asunder' in every age. Jude was helping by placing the distractions his readers were subject to in a wider context, and this is something we can do, too, our context being so different, yet so similar.

Jesus, we thank you for the heritage of learning and wisdom
revealed in the saints through the ages. Amen

GORDON GILES

Be loved

But you, beloved, must remember the predictions of the apostles of our Lord Jesus Christ; for they said to you, 'In the last time there will be scoffers, indulging their own ungodly lusts.' It is these worldly people, devoid of the Spirit, who are causing divisions. But you, beloved, build yourselves up on your most holy faith; pray in the Holy Spirit; keep yourselves in the love of God; look forward to the mercy of our Lord Jesus Christ that leads to eternal life.

Jude turns from reminding his readers of what the Jewish Apocrypha says to what the apostles have said so recently. This might make us feel on firmer ground, 2,000 years later. He is not addressing, and so attacking, those who cause division in the church, but rather warning, encouraging and supporting the faithful who may fall prey to false teaching or depraved behaviour. Thus, he does not so much tell them off as love them, using the word 'beloved' for the third and fourth time in his letter.

Today, if we feel that someone else's behaviour is inappropriate, do we rail about it to others, having a go at them instead? Sometimes we see how people get hot-tempered about whatever a political leader is doing or saying and, unable to criticise that politician directly, they treat anyone who is suspected of being a supporter as though they are that leader. We may choose for whom we vote, but we are not responsible for their actions. We should not necessarily blame someone for being persuaded by an argument.

Jude understands this. He does not 'blame' his readers for being subject to clever or attractive false teaching, but rather calls them 'beloved', reassuring them that he is very much on their side in helping them resist it. The tools he uses are prayer and persuasion. The approach he reminds them to take comes straight from the loving heart of Christianity: build up faith, pray, remember God's love and hold the hope of eternal life. Faith, hope and love; these three, the greatest of which is love.

Jesus, our Saviour, keep us always walking in your way, that we may come at last to eternal joy of union with you in resurrection life. Amen

GORDON GILES

Don't mince words

And have mercy on some who are wavering; save others by snatching them out of the fire; and have mercy on still others with fear, hating even the tunic defiled by their bodies. Now to him who is able to keep you from falling, and to make you stand without blemish in the presence of his glory with rejoicing, to the only God our Saviour, through Jesus Christ our Lord, be glory, majesty, power, and authority, before all time and now and forever. Amen.

Jude's letter is 630 words long. Given how brief it is – less than the word count for two days' worth of *New Daylight* reflections! – it is precise and pithy, pertinent and pointed. He does not mince his few words, seasoning them with love and mercy. For some are in danger of being swayed by spiritual distraction, and their depravity stains their undershirts. Clothes worn by someone diseased are themselves infected. By contrast, one who is undefiled does not have soiled garments, and this is the state to which everyone should aspire before the Lord in judgement. Once again Jude is concerned not just to condemn those who fall, but to implore his readers to help others not fall away from faith. As a final sentence before a closing formulaic ending, it sums up Jude's pastoral, protective and polemical epistle, underpinned by genuine love for all God's people.

Is Jude's world a world away from the here and now? When you read of those whom he is trying to save from error and sin, do particular people come into your mind? Does such a culture and social environment in which God's beloved (that's everyone and anyone) are pulled to and fro morally and spiritually seem like another country, veiled by the mists of time? Or is Jude's message of care for the salvation of all as pertinent and pressing as ever?

Next time you are out and about, look around. Are the people around you in need of salvation, spiritual protection and mercy? Of course they are. Love them and pray for them.

God, as your disciples, help us to reveal your loving mercy to all in spiritual peril, that all may come to know you and be saved. Amen

GORDON GILES

David

So all the generations from Abraham to David are fourteen generations; and from David to the deportation to Babylon, fourteen generations; and from the deportation to Babylon to the Messiah, fourteen generations.
MATTHEW 1:17 (NRSV)

It's probably helped by the fact that he and I share a name, but I have always been fascinated by the stories of King David. The Old Testament portrays him as such a rich character, at times both hero and villain, a man plucked from humble origins to become the one who establishes Israel as a nation.

Over the next fortnight, will be looking at some of the key incidents from his life, from his first calling to the birth of the son who will in time succeed him on the throne. We will follow him through the ups and downs of his relationship with Israel's first king, Saul, and reflect on some of the most memorable tales of his bravery and cowardice, loyalty and treachery. There is probably more about David in the Old Testament than any other figure except Moses. It is this richness, combined with an at times brutal honesty about David's failings, which allows us to see into his life and times in ways that can be informative for our own. Like David, we too are trying to find our way in God's world, a world beset by dangers and disasters as well as opportunities and accomplishments. We too have our friendships and family ties. We may have wider responsibilities in our churches and communities, and find ourselves caught up in struggles for leadership and authority. We may feel chosen or rejected. While it can well be argued that our present society is far more complex than that of a small Middle Eastern kingdom 3,000 years ago, both human nature and God remain unchanged.

David mattered to the writers of the New Testament, and especially to Matthew. In his very first chapter he sets out a genealogy that not only makes explicit the line of descent from Abraham through David to Joseph, the husband of Mary, but also divides it into three equal portions of generations. I hope these reflections over the next two weeks will help each of us to find something in the story of David that matters for us too.

DAVID WALKER

Fruits of faithfulness

So Boaz took Ruth and she became his wife. When they came together, the Lord made her conceive, and she bore a son. Then the women said to Naomi, 'Blessed be the Lord, who has not left you this day without next-of-kin; and may his name be renowned in Israel!'... The women of the neighbourhood gave him a name, saying, 'A son has been born to Naomi.' They named him Obed; he became the father of Jesse, the father of David.

The first mention of David in the Bible is this brief description of his ancestry. Boaz is an Israelite, a man from Bethlehem. He is a relative of Elimelech, the late husband of Naomi, who has returned to Israel from the country of Moab. Ruth, however, is Naomi's Moabite daughter–in–law, and she herself is widowed and has no children. She chooses to leave her own people and their gods in order to accompany Naomi, and so to become faithful to Naomi's God. Poor and with no hope of a dowry, Ruth's expectations are limited. Yet the hand of God intervenes in her life. She meets and marries Boaz.

David, then, is the outcome of an unlikely union, only three generations away from a penniless foreigner. Yet he is also only three generations away from a woman who made firm, positive choices in her life. Ruth prized faithfulness to her dead husband's elderly mother above her own kindred. She travelled in faith, undeterred by her lack of wealth or resources. She freely chose the God of Israel as her Lord.

Ruth did not live to see David, but without Ruth, there would have been no David. The combination of her choices and God's long-term plan serves as a foretaste of the story of Mary, a millennium later. It is a reminder that the Bible is not simply a story about men. Women play a pivotal role. This is also a reminder that the full flowering of what God may be calling any one of us to at this present moment may not be fully visible in our own lifetimes.

God of the future, may I, like Ruth, follow you in my own day and situation, even if the fruits of my faithfulness lie beyond my seeing. Amen

DAVID WALKER

Emerging gifts

Samuel said to Jesse, 'Are all your sons here?' And he said, 'There remains yet the youngest, but he is keeping the sheep.' And Samuel said to Jesse, 'Send and bring him; for we will not sit down until he comes here.' He sent and brought him in. Now he was ruddy, and had beautiful eyes, and was handsome. The Lord said, 'Rise and anoint him; for this is the one.' Then Samuel took the horn of oil, and anointed him in the presence of his brothers; and the spirit of the Lord came mightily upon David from that day forward. Samuel then set out and went to Ramah.

God sends the prophet Samuel to the house of Jesse. Saul has proved unworthy to be king over Israel; instead one of the seven sons of this Bethlehem sheep owner is the Lord's pick as his replacement. But which one? Six older sons are presented, but none is God's choice. David, the last and the least, is not even around; he has been tending the flocks. Yet he is the one God has chosen. From the moment Samuel anoints him, God's Spirit is powerfully upon David, changing him forever.

In my years of ministry, I have seen similar things happen. I have known men and women who, from the moment of their ordination as priests in God's church, have begun to speak and act with new authority and deeper wisdom. I have also seen it with people being appointed to new jobs; from the moment they get the call to say they are the preferred candidate, perhaps months before officially taking up their new position, they are changed. It may not be accompanied by a physical anointing, as Samuel performed with David, but there is a tangible outpouring of God's Spirit.

I doubt David thought of himself as a potential king until that moment. I suspect he may have harboured some doubts as to his destiny for a while after. Yet Samuel's actions opened the way for God to prepare David for the next stage of his journey.

Lord God, help me to know whether there is a David in my own life,
one in whom I recognise emerging gifts, and to whom I can say,
'Might God be calling you?' Amen

DAVID WALKER

Heart songs

So Saul sent messengers to Jesse, and said, 'Send me your son David who is with the sheep.' Jesse took a donkey loaded with bread, a skin of wine, and a kid, and sent them by his son David to Saul. And David came to Saul, and entered his service. Saul loved him greatly, and he became his armour-bearer. Saul sent to Jesse, saying, 'Let David remain in my service, for he has found favour in my sight.' And whenever the evil spirit from God came upon Saul, David took the lyre and played it with his hand, and Saul would be relieved and feel better, and the evil spirit would depart from him.

It does not always remain so, but at first the relationship between David and Saul is strong and positive. David's musical talents are the only thing that can bring peace to the older man when his spirit is troubled. Music can have a powerful effect on mood. Just think of the soundtracks that accompany films and TV series, giving us a taste of the danger, sorrow or joy that the characters on screen are experiencing. Think too of the tunes played through the speakers in shops and supermarkets, calculated to make our shopping experience more pleasant and hence for us to spend a little more than we might otherwise.

Many of the 150 psalms in our Bibles are attested as 'psalms of David'. Whether or not he personally composed the words and tunes, attributing them to him indicates the place he was felt to have held in putting music at the heart of worship. In our own generation, when Covid-19 regulations prevented congregations from singing in churches, this was the matter that most often, and most firmly, came up at meetings I attended between Christian leaders and government.

My own musical talents are negligible, but I know how getting the right musical setting can make a huge difference to my prayers and worship. Augustine reputedly said, 'The one who sings, prays twice.' When feeling distracted, I sometimes play music to accompany my prayers at home, letting modern music devices take the place of David and his lyre.

Lord, whether it be of joy or lament,
grant me a song in my heart today. Amen

DAVID WALKER

Picking battle stones

When the Philistine drew nearer to meet David, David ran quickly towards the battle line to meet the Philistine. David put his hand in his bag, took out a stone, slung it, and struck the Philistine on his forehead; the stone sank into his forehead, and he fell face down on the ground. So David prevailed over the Philistine with a sling and a stone, striking down the Philistine and killing him; there was no sword in David's hand... When the Philistines saw that their champion was dead, they fled.

From sporting conflicts to courtroom battles, the description of some contests as being 'David versus Goliath' remains common usage, even if many may not know its origins. David, the plucky youngster, casts off the heavy armour Saul had offered, along with the king's sword that was too cumbersome for him to handle. He will fight the Philistine champion with just the sling and stones he would have used to ward wild animals off his father's flocks. A single well-aimed strike is sufficient, the giant is vanquished, Israel is saved.

Yet this is far more than a story of human victory against the odds. David responds to his adversary's derisive taunts by asserting it is the 'Lord of hosts, the God of the armies of Israel' (1 Samuel 17:45) who will deliver the fatal blow. He himself is simply God's means to accomplish the victory. This combination of human endeavour and divine will runs as a golden thread through scripture. God works through people who, empowered by his Spirit, can do far beyond what their human capacities alone could achieve. Small forces vanquish mighty armies. Lone prophets, like Elijah, defeat and destroy the priests of Baal. Beyond the scriptural era, a tiny band of disciples becomes a force strong enough to conquer the Roman empire.

David plays his part. He doesn't simply stand and call upon God to destroy his foe with fire from heaven. He uses all the skills and experience he has, choosing his stones carefully, loading his familiar sling. Releasing the projectile, God does the rest. And down the centuries his story echoes.

Lord, help me to discover whether there is some cause or concern today for which I should take the part of David. Amen

DAVID WALKER

Jealous eyes

As they were coming home, when David returned from killing the Philistine, the women came out of all the towns of Israel, singing and dancing, to meet King Saul, with tambourines, with songs of joy, and with musical instruments. And the women sang to one another as they made merry, 'Saul has killed his thousands, and David his tens of thousands.' Saul was very angry, for this saying displeased him. He said, 'They have ascribed to David tens of thousands, and to me they have ascribed thousands; what more can he have but the kingdom?' So Saul eyed David from that day on.

Jealousy lies at the heart of the souring of David's relationship with Saul. The young man's deeds are rated higher than the king's, and that will not do. It may be that Saul already sees David as a potential rival for the throne. He arranges a marriage to one of his daughters, bringing David into the family. But this is not just about kingship, it is about popularity. Saul cannot abide being upstaged in Israel's affections by his armour-bearer and court musician, even if he can now claim him as one of the family.

Even among Jesus' own disciples, jealousy finds its place. If only for a time it sours the relationship between the rest of the twelve and the brothers James and John after they had pressed to be promised seats next to Jesus in his kingdom. Today, jealousy within congregations, or between clergy and church members, can be one of the most forceful inhibitors of the mission and ministry of the church. Sometimes it can be a priest, lacking confidence in their own skills, who limits the opportunities for talented lay members. Sometimes it is rivalries between lay members, vying for positions that carry power or honour and respect or for the attention and affections of the minister.

As with Saul, the root is often insecurity. In some cases, it may be so deep-rooted and enduring that helping the person afflicted can be as unequal a struggle as that of David and Goliath. Though even then, as we heard yesterday, we can remain people of hope.

Heavenly Father, help me both to avoid jealousy in my own life
and to support those injured by the jealousy of others. Amen

DAVID WALKER

Best friendship

Saul spoke to his son Jonathan and to all his servants about killing David. But Saul's son Jonathan took great delight in David... Jonathan spoke well of David to his father Saul, saying to him, 'The king should not sin against his servant David, because he has not sinned against you, and because his deeds have been of good service to you'... Saul heeded the voice of Jonathan; Saul swore, 'As the Lord lives, he shall not be put to death.' So Jonathan called David and related all these things to him. Jonathan then brought David to Saul, and he was in his presence as before.

In many ways the relationship between David and Jonathan is an unlikely alliance. David's destiny will, after all, block Jonathan from succeeding his father to the throne. It stands in sharp contrast with the political marriage that Saul had arranged for David.

Neither David nor Jonathan seeks to manipulate the other for personal advantage. Both exhibit a selflessness and desire for the well-being of the other that reaches its culmination when David hears the news that Jonathan has been killed in battle against the Philistines. He composes a song, known as the 'Song of the Bow', which contains the memorable lines: 'I am distressed for you, my brother Jonathan; greatly beloved were you to me; your love to me was wonderful, passing the love of women' (2 Samuel 1:26). Such is the power and the unpredictability of human affection.

January is the month when I go through all the Christmas cards I have received and read the accompanying letters from which the busyness of the previous few weeks has delayed me. It is an exercise that draws me to challenge myself over how little effort I may have made over the previous year to keep in touch with those from whom time and distance have separated me. More broadly, it challenges me to think of my friends. Have I loved them as much as I should? Have I held their interests ahead of my own, as David and Jonathan did for each other?

Father God, thank you for my own friends, and grant that I may be a better friend in the year ahead. Amen

DAVID WALKER

Waiting to lead

[Saul] came to the sheepfolds beside the road, where there was a cave; and Saul went in to relieve himself. Now David and his men were sitting in the innermost parts of the cave. The men of David said to him, 'Here is the day of which the Lord said to you, "I will give your enemy into your hand, and you shall do to him as it seems good to you."' Then David went and stealthily cut off a corner of Saul's cloak. Afterwards David was stricken to the heart because he had cut off a corner of Saul's cloak. He said to his men, 'The Lord forbid that I should do this thing to my lord, the Lord's anointed, to raise my hand against him; for he is the Lord's anointed.'

The relationship between Saul and David breaks down to the point where the latter is in hiding, accompanied by a small group of loyal companions. Chance, or maybe God's providence, suddenly places Saul at David's mercy. Yet rather than exploit the opportunity, David merely cuts off a piece of Saul's cloak, providing proof for later that he could have killed him. It is not that David is a man opposed to violence; as the women sang, he had killed many Philistines over the course of Israel's wars. Rather, he recognises that Saul still carries the authority of one anointed by God as king, even if it is an authority he is exercising poorly. It will be for God to remove Saul from power, not David. And when it happens, it will be at the hands of the Philistines, not one of his own subjects.

This story has uncomfortable echoes with recent times. In both Iraq and Libya, we have seen the violent removal of a tyrant create a vacuum of power which something equally bad, if not worse, swiftly filled. Had David murdered Saul, the likely outcome would have been prolonged civil war, weakening Israel until it became easy prey to its enemies. Instead, David shows patience. His time will come when God is ready. His eventual accession to the throne will come at far less a cost to human life.

Lord Jesus, you waited 30 years to begin your public ministry; grant me patience when I am called to abide a little longer. Amen

DAVID WALKER

Decision time

After this David inquired of the Lord, 'Shall I go up into any of the cities of Judah?' The Lord said to him, 'Go up.' David said, 'To which shall I go up?' He said, 'To Hebron.' So David went up there, along with his two wives, Ahinoam of Jezreel, and Abigail the widow of Nabal of Carmel. David brought up the men who were with him, every one with his household; and they settled in the towns of Hebron. Then the people of Judah came, and there they anointed David king over the house of Judah.

Last week we looked at the story of David in the years before he became king. Now our attention turns to his time upon the throne. With Saul dead, David's own tribe, Judah, swiftly proclaims him monarch. By now David is 30 years old and the young shepherd boy first anointed by Samuel has grown into a seasoned warrior. He will need those skills in the years to come. The enemies of Israel will never be far away. Moreover, the greatest challenges to his rule will not be external. Powerful forces from within Israel's twelve tribes will seek to seize his throne. His immediate opponents are those who throw their allegiance behind Ishbaal, Saul's son, but later he will be confronted by the ambitions of Absalom, one of his own offspring. There will be times of relative peace and tranquillity, and periods when he is forced to flee for his life. And yet he will survive as king for four decades and die peacefully, having chosen Solomon from among his sons to be his successor.

David begins in the way he seeks to continue throughout his reign, seeking God's will and intention for him, before he takes one of the biggest decisions of his life. He does not pretend that his own wisdom will be sufficient. Sometimes, in the years to come, he will seek God's will through consulting a prophet, such as Nathan. Here and now, we are not told how he discovers God's will. The means matters less than the fact.

Lord, help me to abide in this truth: that the major decisions of my life, and even many minor ones, are made better for being taken in the light of my relationship with you. Amen

DAVID WALKER

The shepherd king

Then all the tribes of Israel came to David at Hebron, and said, 'Look, we are your bone and flesh. For some time, while Saul was king over us, it was you who led out Israel and brought it in. The Lord said to you: It is you who shall be shepherd of my people Israel, you who shall be ruler over Israel.' So all the elders of Israel came to the king at Hebron; and King David made a covenant with them at Hebron before the Lord, and they anointed David king over Israel.

The most powerful imagery is often drawn from everyday life. Stories that resonate with our personal experience are more likely to move us than ones that speak of lives very different from our own. The tribes of Israel formed from a loose collection of sheep farmers. At first semi-nomadic, they later settled in the hills of what would become their kingdom. It was some time until they were strong enough to capture the towns and cities. Jerusalem itself only fell in the early years of David's reign. Hence, it should not be surprising that when they look to define what sort of role a king should exercise, the people of Israel think in terms of shepherds looking after their flock.

It is an image that needs to be stripped of any sentimentality. We are worlds away from the French queen Marie Antoinette playing at being a shepherdess in the grounds of her royal palace. The shepherds that David's generation knew lived tough lives, out in the worst of weathers, protecting their sheep from wild animals and sheep-stealers, rescuing them when they fell into danger and coaxing them into their sheepfolds for shelter. These are the qualities Israel seeks in a king: someone to care for them and protect them, to see that they have adequate supplies and shelter and are safe from assailants, and to lead them into new pastures when the old become exhausted. Shepherds may not be so much of a feature in our own society, but these principles of leadership stand the test of time and culture.

Heavenly Father, grant that, in whatever leadership roles I may be called, I can draw strength and wisdom from the example of David, the shepherd king. Amen

DAVID WALKER

David's dance

So David went and brought up the ark of God from the house of Obed-edom to the city of David with rejoicing; and when those who bore the ark of the Lord had gone six paces, he sacrificed an ox and a fatling. David danced before the Lord with all his might; David was girded with a linen ephod. So David and all the house of Israel brought up the ark of the Lord with shouting, and with the sound of the trumpet.

In a society that vehemently rejected images of God as alien to its faith, the ark of God was the most sacred physical object known. David had already failed once to bring it to Jerusalem, aborting the journey when one of those accompanying it was killed. Temporarily lodged in the home of Obed-edom, its presence had brought that household great blessings. So David feels great joy when he can bring it into his new capital city at last. His dancing is so unrestrained that it embitters his wife Michal against him, for his lack of appropriate royal dignity. But for David, to have this symbol of the presence and blessings of God with him matters far more than his personal decorum.

I love this story, because it shows us David the man responding with his whole self to the God he worships. My own spiritual tradition is relatively restrained. I need to be reminded that my body can play as much a part in praising God as my heart and my mind. And even though I may not be drawn to the unrestrained dancing of David, I try to use my posture and physical movements as part of my response to God. Sometimes I will pray with my hands open, ready to receive whatever God desires to place in them. When I sing some worship songs, I move my hands or arms in response to the lyrics, raising them to praise God or making the sign of the cross when Christ's passion is mentioned. It is not necessary to be a member of a charismatic church to benefit from allowing one's whole body to be drawn into worship.

Holy Spirit, be at work within me, that by your power I may worship the Lord in body, mind and spirit. Amen

DAVID WALKER

Power corrupts

In the spring of the year, the time when kings go out to battle, David sent Joab with his officers and all Israel with him; they ravaged the Ammonites, and besieged Rabbah. But David remained at Jerusalem. It happened, late one afternoon, when David rose from his couch and was walking about on the roof of the king's house, that he saw from the roof a woman bathing; the woman was very beautiful. David sent someone to inquire about the woman. It was reported, 'This is Bathsheba daughter of Eliam, the wife of Uriah the Hittite.' So David sent messengers to fetch her, and she came to him, and he lay with her.

The very fact that David remains in Jerusalem in the spring season, when kings should lead their armies in person, reflects badly on him. They are facing danger, besieging Rabbah. He has time to take an afternoon nap, stroll about on the flat roof of his dwelling and then indulge his passions with the wife of one of his absent warriors. As the adage goes, power corrupts, and David proves himself to be no exception.

The temptation for all leaders is to see themselves as somehow deserving exemption from the rules that apply to everyone else. No doubt David's heavy responsibilities wearied him, making him feel entitled to take some rest. Moreover, with much to do in establishing his capital city, he had plausible reasons for not accompanying his army. The prohibition of adultery would have been harder for him to simply set aside. Did he blame Bathsheba for provocatively bathing where he could see her? Or did he feel his royal status gave him the right to have any woman he wanted?

Back in the 1970s, at a time of high annual inflation, a UK opinion poll showed that around three quarters of those responding believed that wage increases ought to be capped by law. An even higher percentage, however, thought their own profession should be exempt. You don't have to be a king to believe that you can bend the rules for your own benefit, especially if you think you can get away with it.

Almighty Father, help me to examine my own practices and attitudes, and to weed out false claims of exceptionalism. Amen

DAVID WALKER

Reputational risks

In the morning David wrote a letter to Joab, and sent it by the hand of Uriah. In the letter he wrote, 'Set Uriah in the forefront of the hardest fighting, and then draw back from him, so that he may be struck down and die.' As Joab was besieging the city, he assigned Uriah to the place where he knew there were valiant warriors. The men of the city came out and fought with Joab; and some of the servants of David among the people fell. Uriah the Hittite was killed as well.

David's downfall lies in Bathsheba falling pregnant while her husband is away. He finds himself embarking on a course of action that has been repeated so many times in human history: he plots a cover-up. Uriah is invited back to Jerusalem, given strong drink and encouraged to sleep with his wife. The plan fails when Uriah refuses to enter his home, considering it improper while the rest of the army is out in the field. Thwarted once, David embarks on an even more reprehensible course, arranging for Uriah to be killed in battle. This time the scheme succeeds. Nobody will ever know. Except, for once in his life, David has reckoned without God.

From church safeguarding failures to the shortcomings of politicians, attempts to cover up wrongdoing compound and exacerbate the original offence. While it remains a principle of law that no one should be compelled to testify against themselves, there is a world of difference between that human right and deliberately disguising personal or corporate failure.

Both individuals and institutions are accountable to the laws and morals of the societies in which they find themselves. Yet, as with the original offence, the justification for covering up lies in some sense of exceptionalism. David may regret his adultery, but he sees himself, and his survival as king, as more important than issues of justice. In the same way, religious leaders have covered up abuse to protect the reputation of the church, thereby feeling they are guarding the gospel itself. Political leaders may consider the good that will follow from their retaining public approval as trumping all other considerations. As indeed may we.

Loving Lord, give me the courage to never consider that
preserving my reputation outweighs the truth. Amen

DAVID WALKER

35

Worship in grief

The Lord struck the child that Uriah's wife bore to David, and it became very ill. David therefore pleaded with God for the child; David fasted, and went in and lay all night on the ground… On the seventh day the child died… Then David rose from the ground, washed, anointed himself, and changed his clothes. He went into the house of the Lord, and worshipped; he then went to his own house; and when he asked, they set food before him and he ate.

David's behaviour seems to defy all normal human sentiment. He fasts and prays while the infant remains alive, but as soon as the child dies, he appears to act as though nothing has happened. When his servants query this unusual behaviour, his response is that he had been pleading for God to spare the child. With the baby dead, such prayers and fasting no longer serve any purpose. Logical though that may be, it strikes now, as it did then, as incredibly cold. Bathsheba mourns the death of her child, while David seems impervious. Yet neither does he follow the course of many who have prayed in extremity, but then ceased to do so afterwards. Far from disowning the God who has failed to grant his request, one of David's first actions, on ceasing his lament, is to go and worship.

I have spent my adult life seeking to understand both the scriptures and human behaviour, yet David's reaction still perplexes me. How can he care so much for the life of the child and yet not mourn their death? Yet perhaps the message is that attempting to fully understand how other people process loss and bereavement is futile. David's behaviour, complicated by both adultery and murder, is not something to analyse. Maybe instead we need to focus on a much clearer message that the story contains, that despite this most tragic sequence of events – adultery, murder and death – David and God are far from finished with one another, and through that divine and human cooperation, God's purposes for Israel and for humanity will continue to roll forward.

Lord, thank you that no matter how far I fall, I can never
fall out of your loving arms. Amen

DAVID WALKER

Solomon

Then David consoled his wife Bathsheba, and went to her, and lay with her; and she bore a son, and he named him Solomon. The Lord loved him, and sent a message by the prophet Nathan; so he named him Jedidiah, because of the Lord.

Solomon is named only twice in the second book of Samuel. First, simply in a list of names, and then with this brief mention of his birth. Yet the story bursts with promise. From the beginning of his life, we are told that the Lord loved him; indeed, he is given a special name, Jedidiah, which translates as 'beloved of the Lord'. David has been promised that because of his faithfulness to God, unlike Saul, he will be the father of a dynasty of kings. Though it is not yet made explicit, this child is the one who will ultimately succeed him.

Newly born Solomon has done nothing to merit such love. Indeed, given David's relationship with Bathsheba, one might expect another of David's sons to receive special blessing. But Solomon it is. This stands as a reminder that God's love precedes anything we do to merit it. We are loved simply for ourselves. Divine grace is unearned. This message will ultimately be made clear in Jesus Christ. How to respond to this undeserved love will be for each human individual to determine for themselves, but the love itself remains steadfast.

Yet within God's plan particular individuals may be singled out. Such a choosing may come, as it did for David, as a young man. Others, like Solomon are set apart from the moment of birth. This is not to say that the earthly course of any individual is predetermined. Endowed with free will, we can choose to respond positively to God's promptings, or otherwise. As we take our leave of David, both he and the babe in his arms have far to travel. Both will have many choices to make; getting some right and others wrong. But both will play their part in God's overall work of loving his creation. As will I. As will you.

Heavenly Father, may I rest secure in the knowledge that you have loved me every moment of my existence, and always will. Amen

DAVID WALKER

Deep waters of discipleship: Luke 4—6

Luke's gospel is an invaluable source of insight into Jesus' mission and vision, and during the next two weeks we will accompany him through the first crucial period of his earthly ministry. We will be invited to not just observe but also participate in that ministry and reflect on what it is asking of us personally, two millennia later.

Our journey begins in the wilderness. We learn that the Spirit leads Jesus while in the wilderness, an assurance in itself that the same Spirit will be there to lead us too, as we navigate the wilderness parts of our own lives and face the temptations that beset us.

It is said that what doesn't break us makes us stronger, and Jesus returns from the wilderness strengthened by the Spirit and by his resistance to the temptations and ready to begin his public ministry by proclaiming in the synagogue that the time is at hand for the coming of the kingdom.

And from the beginning, the gospel message attracts opposition. Where a bright light shines, there will always be a shadow. Almost immediately, Jesus is hounded out of the synagogue because those who hear him don't like his message and its implicit challenge to their righteous self-assurance. The opposition continues when he heals the man with the withered hand on the sabbath, incurring the wrath of the scribes and Pharisees, but also challenging us today to reflect on whether we allow rules and regulations to blind us to a greater vision. The call of Levi similarly compels us to confront our prejudices and deal with our tendency to self-righteousness.

These three chapters are rich in parables, guiding us in how to live in a way that reflects the kingdom of God. We are urged to not judge others, to love those who would harm us, and to build our spiritual lives on solid foundations in a world where there are so many treacherous quicksands to pull us away from our true course and suck us into the shallows.

Again and again Jesus calls us to listen to his teaching, but then to put his words into action in our own lives as we respond to his personal call to each of us to risk the deeper waters of discipleship.

MARGARET SILF

Temptation and resistance

[Jesus] was led by the Spirit in the wilderness, where for forty days he was tempted by the devil… 'If you are the Son of God, command this stone to become a loaf of bread.' Jesus answered him, 'It is written, "One does not live by bread alone."' Then the devil… showed him… all the kingdoms of the world… 'To you I will give their glory and all this authority… if you, then, will worship me…' Jesus answered him, 'It is written "Worship the Lord your God, and serve only him."' Then the devil… placed him on the pinnacle of the temple, saying to him, 'If you are the Son of God, throw yourself down from here…' Jesus answered him, 'It is said, "Do not put the Lord your God to the test."'

We could see Jesus' temptations as a cosmic confrontation between good and evil, and the ultimate triumph of good. This is certainly one layer of meaning in this encounter. Its full power, however, lies in its application to our own experience. Jesus is fully human and therefore fully exposed to temptation, as we are ourselves. The difference lies in his ability to resist.

Jesus is hungry and knows he could force nature to yield bread from stones, but this would be serving his own needs and denying the greater truth that life is about more than physical satisfaction. Events throughout history show how easily a dictator can manipulate a starving people into colluding with great evil by promising the short-term relief of food and jobs.

Jesus could take secular control over all the world by focusing on his own personal power. Secular leaders often put their own power and glory above the common good. Jesus asserts that the only ultimate authority lies with God.

Jesus could prove his power instantly by leaping unharmed from the pinnacle, but this would be a mere circus stunt that would debase the true nature of his mission. How readily we press God, like impatient children, to prove himself to us.

This cosmic confrontation plays out, in us, through the constant struggle between our ego-selves and our true selves. The ego-self says, 'Me first!' The true self responds, 'God first!'

What personal temptations do you wrestle with in your inner wilderness?

MARGARET SILF

The Fourth Sunday of Epiphany 39

Fulfilled in your hearing

[Jesus] stood up to read, and the scroll of the prophet Isaiah was given to him. He unrolled the scroll and found the place where it was written: 'The Spirit of the Lord is upon me, because he has anointed me to bring good news to the poor. He has sent me to proclaim release to the captives and recovery of sight to the blind, to let the oppressed go free, to proclaim the year of the Lord's favour'… The eyes of all in the synagogue were fixed on him. The he began to say to them, 'Today this scripture has been fulfilled in your hearing.'

I once had the privilege of briefly accompanying a chaplain to seafarers in a busy port in northern England. I have never forgotten his devotion and passion in championing the seafarers who passed through the port and who were often in need of support. We depend on these sailors to bring us our food and other essentials. My companion knew all too well the hardship, isolation and injustices they suffer in doing so.

For example, they had had no contact with their families for months; the chaplain arranged access to computers on shore, for them to see and speak to their loved ones. Sometimes their wages were not being paid to their families; the chaplain reported this to the port authorities and insisted on justice. On one occasion he asked a passing crew what they would like to do in their brief sojourn on shore. 'We would love to walk on grass,' they said. He took them to a local park and these sailors, who had known nothing but a rolling steel deck beneath their feet for months, rejoiced to walk barefoot on the grass. 'You would have thought I'd given them the earth,' he commented humbly. 'That's exactly what you did,' I said.

The chaplain gave sight to the blind through a computer link. He set them free from oppression by demanding justice on their behalf. He brought them good news in the form of kindness, care and love in action. This scripture is being fulfilled all around us in many different ways.

In what ways can you see this scripture being fulfilled in today's world?

MARGARET SILF

The prophet from next door

All spoke well of him and were amazed at the gracious words that came from his mouth. They said, 'Is not this Joseph's son?'… He said to them, 'Truly I tell you, no prophet is accepted in the prophet's home town'… When they heard this, all in the synagogue were filled with rage. They got up, drove him out of the town, and led him to the brow of the hill on which their town was built, so that they might hurl him off the cliff. But he passed through the midst of them and went on his way.

Why is it often easier to recognise truth when it comes from a stranger who is removed from our everyday lives than when we are confronted with it in the midst of the familiar? Prophets, we think, are unlikely to live in our street or go the to the school we went to. Hard truths are more palatable when we feel able to distance ourselves from their impact. The prophet who lives next door threatens our complacency. Maybe this was how the people in the synagogue were reacting to the truth that Jesus was teaching.

Jesus blows their cover, compelling them to take his teaching to heart and live it out in the real world he shares with them. Their admiration dissolves as soon as they realise he can see through them. It turns to rage. This man must be silenced. It is one thing to admire the speaker at the podium; it is quite another to internalise his teaching and live it out. And perhaps for us, adulation fades when we are challenged to apply what we are hearing to our own neighbourhood and our own relationships.

I had a dear friend who was also something of a prophet, though he would have denied this. He was a man of deep integrity and much admired. His books were widely read. People flocked to his workshops. But some of them flocked out again when his teaching cut too close to the bone. They walked out in protest. They complained to the bishop. They gave him a hard time. They banned him from their churches. How easily 'Hosanna!' turns to 'Crucify!'

Who are our prophets today, and are we really listening to them?

MARGARET SILF

Into deeper water

Once while Jesus was standing beside the lake of Gennesaret, and the crowd was pressing in on him to hear the word of God, he saw two boats there at the shore of the lake; the fishermen had gone out of them and were washing their nets. He got into one of the boats, the one belonging to Simon, and asked him to put out a little way from the shore. Then he sat down and taught the crowds from the boat. When he had finished speaking, he said to Simon, 'Put out into the deep water and let down your nets for a catch.' Simon answered, 'Master, we have worked all night long but have caught nothing. Yet if you say so, I will let down the nets.'

Can you imagine this scene at the lakeside? I often wonder how I would have reacted if Jesus had simply stepped into my boat and asked me to make space for him so that he could more effectively address the crowd. Yet Jesus doesn't just want to borrow the boat. He also wants to give some crucial instruction to the men who would one day bring the gospel to future crowds.

The instruction has two parts. First, Jesus needs to 'put out a little way from the shore'. The small distance between listeners and teacher enables him to be heard and seen by many more people. Second, he then turns directly to Simon and sends him into deeper water to continue fishing. All of us who seek to follow Jesus will hear him invite us to sail into deeper waters. What will this mean for us? One of the greatest hazards to shipping is not the deep but the shallow water, where a boat can easily become stranded. This is also true of our spiritual journeying. There is a constant temptation to stay in safe and shallow waters and not venture out of our depth. Yet it is wisely said that we will never discover new lands without leaving the shore. Simon and his companions are being invited to discover new horizons beyond their present understanding and new depths of trust within themselves.

What does it mean to you to be invited by Jesus into deeper waters?

MARGARET SILF

Fishers of people

When they had done this, they caught so many fish that their nets were beginning to break. So they signalled to their partners in the other boat to come and help them. And they came and filled both boats, so that they began to sink. But when Simon Peter saw it, he fell down at Jesus' knees, saying 'Go away from me, Lord, for I am a sinful man!'... Then Jesus said to Simon, 'Do not be afraid; from now on you will be catching people.' When they had brought their boats to shore, they left everything and followed him.

Simon, if you recall, had complained that they had caught nothing all night, but he had nevertheless obeyed Jesus' instruction to put down the nets in deeper water. Now they had caught so many fish that the nets were in danger of breaking and they needed to call for help to haul in the catch. Something has shifted completely because of the presence of Jesus, who, rather mysteriously, tells them that in future they will be fishing for people.

We are very familiar with this gospel story. For most of my life the call to be 'fishers of people' didn't really resonate, as I had no experience whatsoever of angling or any idea how to go about it. This changed when one day a visiting minister came to the university chaplaincy to which I belonged. His message was so simple, so obvious, yet so enlightening. 'Jesus called them to become fishers of people,' he said, 'because they were already fishing fish.' In other words, Jesus calls us to use and develop the skills, gifts and experience we already have in the service of the kingdom. 'What would Jesus have said to *you*?' he added, then gave us a few minutes of silence to reflect on this question. At the time I was a technical author in the computer industry. During that reflection time I could almost hear Jesus whispering to me with a smile, 'I could give you something much more interesting to write about.'

The hard part is what they did next: left everything and followed him.

In the light of the minister's question, where do you think Jesus might be asking you to go fishing?

MARGARET SILF

Social leprosy

Once, when he was in one of the cities, there was a man covered with leprosy. When he saw Jesus, he bowed with his face to the ground and begged him, 'Lord, if you choose, you can make me clean.' Then Jesus stretched out his hand, touched him, and said, 'I do choose. Be made clean.' Immediately the leprosy left him. And he ordered him to tell no one. 'Go,' he said, 'and show yourself to the priest, and, as Moses commanded, make an offering for your cleansing, for a testimony to them.'

There are effective treatments today for the physical disease of leprosy. There are, however, many less visible ways of being a 'leper' that are harder to heal. Every day there are new revelations of the marginalisation of groups of people who, for whatever reason, do not fit into what their culture considers 'clean'.

Today's reading describes an exchange between Jesus and a leper of his own time. Notice how the leper approaches Jesus, bowing low, his face obscured and in an attitude of supplication. This seems to be a man who is used to being shunned and possibly abused. Yet he comes in faith to Jesus, believing that if Jesus so chooses, he can free him of his untouchable status.

At first the leper's words to Jesus seem strange: Jesus can make him clean, but the leper says, *if he chooses to do so*. We might want to reassure him that of course Jesus chooses, because Jesus, in his own words, comes that we might have life and life in all its fullness (John 10:10). There is surely no question about whether Jesus chooses to heal this man.

There is, however, an urgent question being directed to *us*. In our interactions with modern-day 'lepers', those forced to the edges of our society, will we choose to free them from the unjust stigma of being 'unclean'? They are out there, bowed low, eyes downcast, accustomed to feeling unacceptable. They can't free themselves. We can help free them. Can we say, with Jesus, 'I do choose. Be welcome'?

Who are the marginalised social 'lepers' in our world today?
How might we help to free them from their lives of exclusion?

MARGARET SILF

Let down

One day, while he was teaching, Pharisees and teachers of the law were sitting nearby… Just then some men came carrying a paralysed man on a bed. They were trying to bring him in and lay him before Jesus; but finding no way to bring him in because of the crowd, they went up on the roof and let him down with his bed through the tiles into the middle of the crowd in front of Jesus. When he saw their faith, he said, 'Friend, your sins are forgiven you… I say to you, stand up and take your bed and go to your home.' Immediately he stood up before them, took what he had been lying on, and went to his home, glorifying God.

This is one of my favourite gospel stories for several reasons. First, it is a story of overcoming serious obstacles to achieve a goal. It seemed impossible for these friends to push through the crowds of people to bring their paralysed companion close to Jesus. There are many kinds of throng that can block our way to God: busyness, demands, distractions. Is anything crowding out your focus on God right now?

Once on the roof the friends would have had to remove a section of the roof to gain access to Jesus. Sometimes the structures we build, whether in personal relationships, in society or in religious institutions, can also become barriers. We may need to break through such barriers, though if so, we should do so with care and with prayer. Are you facing any barriers like this?

And finally, the paralysed man arrived at the feet of Jesus by being, quite literally, 'let down'; but 'let down' can also imply being failed. None of us like to be let down by friends or to feel we have let them down. Sometimes it feels as though life itself has let us down and fate is conspiring against us. It is surely no coincidence that it is often at times like these when we are most likely to draw closer to God. This story reminds us that being let down is not always bad news.

Our vulnerability can turn barriers into bridges
and make the impossible possible.

MARGARET SILF

Tax collectors and sinners

After this he went out and saw a tax-collector named Levi, sitting at the tax booth; and he said to him, 'Follow me.' And he got up, left everything, and followed him. Then Levi gave a great banquet for him in his house; and there was a large crowd of tax-collectors and others sitting at the table with them. The Pharisees and their scribes were complaining to his disciples, saying, 'Why do you eat and drink with tax-collectors and sinners?' Jesus answered, 'Those who are well have no need of a physician, but those who are sick; I have come to call not the righteous but sinners to repentance.'

Once, while staying at a rainforest retreat in Australia, which had been founded and then run by succeeding generations of the same family, I noticed a gap in their gallery of forebears. When I asked what had happened to this individual, I was told, 'We don't mention him.' I wondered why. Rather embarrassed, they told me, 'He was transported to Australia for killing a tax inspector.'

Fortunately Jesus adopts a radically different approach to tax collectors. Today, just as in Jesus' time, some occupations are less popular than others. We tend to nurse a special and very unfair grievance against those whose job it is to persuade us to pay our dues. Few of us are eager to pay taxes, even though we know perfectly well they are the means of funding the public services we value, such as health and education.

Jesus accepts no such intolerance and immediately invites Levi to follow him, making it clear there is no place in the kingdom for prejudice of any kind. In response, Levi overflows with gratitude by throwing a huge party, which Jesus clearly relishes, only to be reproached for associating with those of whom the self-righteous scribes and Pharisees disapprove.

We must all count ourselves among the 'tax collectors and sinners', regardless of our occupation and social status. But this does mean we are all welcome at the party, because it is for us that Jesus came.

Self-righteousness is the only barrier keeping us away from the feast where we are welcome guests and Jesus the welcoming host. How can you put self-righteousness aside today?

MARGARET SILF

New wineskins

[Jesus] also told them a parable: 'No one tears a piece from a new garment and sews it on an old garment; otherwise the new will be torn, and the piece from the new will not match the old. And no one puts new wine into old wineskins; otherwise the new wine will burst the skins and will be spilled, and the skins will be destroyed. But new wine must be put into fresh wineskins. And no one after drinking old wine desires new wine, but says, "The old is good."'

This parable always leads me to reflect on the tensions between generations. Perhaps it is because of the images of 'tearing away' and 'bursting out' – phrases sometimes used to criticise the behaviour of the young.

The life cycles of butterflies can help us understand this parable. They fly for thousands of miles – for example, from Mexico to Canada and back – and yet have a very brief lifespan. The length of their journey would equate to several butterfly lifetimes, so they fly in relays. The first cohort flies to a known gathering place where they lay their eggs, which then hatch and metamorphose into the next generation, who then fly on into the second lap of the journey, and so on, until the fourth generation reaches the destination. If the later generations were forced to repeat the same stretch as their parents, there would be no progress. Likewise if we try to force the new wine of our young people into our old patterns of life, there will be no progress.

This parable has something important to teach us about our present intergenerational frictions. Just as you cannot put new wine in old wineskins, so too you cannot put old heads on young shoulders. If we try to shape the young in our own mould, they will tear away and their energy, like spilled wine, will be wasted. Life is a relay journey. The young must forge new paths forward, while honouring the legacy of those who have gone before. Their elders in their turn must trust the young to continue the journey they themselves began.

With mutual respect and trust, the 'old wine' and the 'new wineskins' can journey together to make a future more faithful and fruitful than the past.

MARGARET SILF

47

The spirit of sabbath

On another sabbath [Jesus] entered the synagogue and taught, and there was a man there whose right hand was withered. The scribes and the Pharisees watched him to see whether he would cure on the sabbath, so that they might find an accusation against him. Even though he knew what they were thinking, he said to the man who had the withered hand, 'Come and stand here.' He got up and stood there. Then Jesus said to them, 'I ask you, is it lawful to do good or to do harm on the sabbath, to save life or to destroy it?' After looking around at all of them, he said to him, 'Stretch out your hand.' He did so, and his hand was restored. But they were filled with fury and discussed with one another what they might do to Jesus.

What a powerful contrast there is in this incident in the synagogue! On the one hand we see the scribes and the Pharisees in a huddle, conspiring on how to bring Jesus down. When we are looking for a reason to incriminate someone, we easily become secretive and sinister. This is not the spirit of the sabbath.

On the other hand we find Jesus openly defying the plot against him, and simply doing what his whole nature demands, bringing healing, forgiveness and peace. And alongside him the man with the withered hand, through Jesus' touch, is now able to stretch it out and be restored to health.

We might go on to imagine the joy of the healed man set against the rage of the frustrated scribes and Pharisees. They had plotted in secret to indict Jesus of infringing the sabbath rules. Jesus, by contrast, calls the man out to stand alongside him facing those who wanted to prevent his healing as he asks the simple, searching question: what does the sabbath ask of us, to do good or to do harm?

Of course the answer is obvious, yet still today we so easily allow our best potential to be undermined by our self-imposed rules and regulations, blinded by bureaucracy to the bigger vision of what it means to be fully human.

May we too stretch out our hands to embrace
all that the gospel is calling us to be.

MARGARET SILF

Loving the enemy

'But I say to you that listen, Love your enemies, do good to those who hate you, bless those who curse you, pray for those who abuse you. If anyone strikes you on the cheek, offer the other also; and from anyone who takes your coat do not withhold even your shirt. Give to everyone who begs from you; and if anyone takes away your goods, do not ask for them again. Do to others as you would have them do to you.'

For so many years I have heard these words and outwardly acknowledged their truth and wisdom. Inwardly, however, if I am honest, I have thought that to love our enemies in practice is an ideal that is far out of reach. I might have left it at that had I not come across some invaluable guidance in a book by M. Scott Peck, who suggests that 'love is not an emotion. Love is a decision.'

We can't manufacture an emotion but we *can* make a decision. Our emotions are not under our control; our decisions are. I realised that while it is impossible to *feel* love for our enemies, we do have the option to *choose* to do the more loving thing for them. This doesn't make it easy, but it does bring the command within human reach.

There was a very harsh winter one year. A young woman lived next door to the neighbour from hell, who made trouble for her at every opportunity. A fence of hostility bristled between their gardens. There was absolutely no love between them. Then the snow came. The elderly lady was housebound. Her young neighbour couldn't just ignore her.

Risking a tirade of unpleasantness she knocked on her neighbour's door, offering help. Over the following weeks, as the snow melted, their relationship gradually thawed too. Grumpiness gave way to gratitude in the older lady's heart. The younger woman did not feel love for her difficult neighbour, but when she offered to get the shopping, she was choosing to do the more loving thing. She was obeying the commandment without realising it.

Choosing the more loving way forward is a decision we are all free to make in small ways and great, regardless of how we may feel.

MARGARET SILF

The log in my eye

'Do not judge, and you will not be judged; do not condemn, and you will not be condemned. Forgive, and you will be forgiven; give, and it will be given to you. A good measure, pressed down, shaken together, running over, will be put into your lap; for the measure you give will be the measure you get back... Why do you see the speck in your neighbour's eye, but do not notice the log in your own eye?... First take the log out of your own eye, and then you will see clearly to take the speck out of your neighbour's eye.'

It was coffee break time, and a colleague and I were looking down from the seventh floor of our high-rise office building, from which point we had a clear view of the entrance foyer at ground level.

A rather fragile looking young man approached the revolving doors, clearly struggling with getting inside. His limp suggested that he had impaired mobility. As he stood uncertainly at the entrance, another man came bouncing out of the revolving door, and pushed straight past him, almost knocking him over, and throwing a perfunctory 'Sorry' over his shoulder as he went.

I turned to my colleague, shocked at what we had seen. 'Did you see that?' I asked. 'That man was in such a hurry he almost sent that poor guy flying.' 'Yes,' my colleague replied, 'I saw it too, and it looked really bad, but I know that second man who came out in such haste. I know him, and he's blind.'

I was stunned into silence, and these words from scripture immediately came back to me and hit me hard. How could I have been so quick to judge, when I had no knowledge of the facts? My colleague's quiet understanding put me to shame.

This incident happened many years ago, but the lesson has never left me. I had been ready that day to take the speck out of the eye of a complete stranger, but I myself was more blind than the man who had almost caused the accident.

May I have the grace to open my eyes and my heart
before I open my mouth.

MARGARET SILF

Good source, good fruit

'No good tree bears bad fruit, nor again does a bad tree bear good fruit; for each tree is known by its own fruit. Figs are not gathered from thorns, nor are grapes picked from a bramble bush. The good person out of the good treasure of the heart produces good, and the evil person out of the evil treasure produces evil; for it is out of the abundance of the heart that the mouth speaks.'

It had been a tough day on retreat, and I was more than usually aware of my own failures and inadequacies. I wandered discontentedly through the orchard and came to a standstill in front of a gnarled and withered-looking apple tree. On one shaky branch I noticed a healthy ripe apple. It felt as though God was assuring me that if a tree has healthy fruit, it must be, at its heart, a healthy tree. I felt incredibly encouraged.

The memory of this incident has never left me. Since then when I feel discouraged, I try to look, gratefully, at any fruit my life might be bearing and trust this promise that good fruit can only grow out of a good source. There must be some good soil in my heart for that fruit to have grown. The more we nourish the good fruit of our hearts, the more it will grow and multiply.

More importantly, when I meet other people, especially those who seem to be doing more harm than good, I try to notice any good fruit, however small, that is growing on the tree of their life. Quakers affirm that 'there is that of God in everyone'. While this can occasionally be hard to believe, I find that when I look for the good fruit, either in myself or in others, I will find it, however hidden. Where there is one 'good apple', there will surely be more. God rejoices in every good fruit that grows on our life's tree and uses it to nourish a spiritually hungry world.

May our eyes be opened to recognise and nourish good fruit
in ourselves and in each other.

MARGARET SILF

Firm foundations

'Why do you call me "Lord, Lord", and do not do what I tell you? I will show you what someone is like who comes to me, hears my words, and acts on them. That one is like a man building a house, who dug deeply and laid the foundation on rock; when a flood arose, the river burst against that house but could not shake it, because it had been well built. But the one who hears and does not act is like a man who built a house on the ground without a foundation. When the river burst against it, immediately it fell, and great was the ruin of that house.'

Anyone thinking of building a house is well advised to obtain a thorough survey of the ground before embarking on the work. Former neighbours of mine purchased a plot of land and began to dig the foundations but couldn't find solid ground. In the end they had to lay more bricks under the ground to establish a firm foundation.

Jesus warns us, in this parable, about the crucial importance of building our lives on firm foundations. This, he says, means not simply hearing his teaching, but actually applying it in our everyday lives. It is not enough to be full of admiration for the architect's plans if we don't use them to build the house.

We have to go deep to establish a firm foundation for our spiritual life too and resist the temptation to build on the shallower, shifting ground that the world constantly offers us. Life's superficial attractions can be swept away overnight when the winds of circumstance change. Even things we think are stable, such as health, employment and trusted relationships, are vulnerable to unexpected storms.

How do we reach this solid foundation in our spiritual lives, so that they will withstand the storms and not be swept away by the flood? Jesus makes it very clear. We are not just to pay lip service to all he teaches but strive to live in such a way that our lives are wholly centred on his truth.

The more turbulent the times, the greater the need for deep foundations.

MARGARET SILF

Praise and warnings: Revelation 5—9

 When I was training for ordination, I was privileged to be among students from across the world. Some had come from countries where it was difficult to be entirely open about their faith. Letters might be opened, words weaponised and used against you, and the abiding fear was real that you were not completely safe from interference from governments hostile to or suspicious of your faith. I learned that one way such students responded was to write in code. Simple phrases would mean a great deal more to the recipient of the letter than any third party attempting to intercept it, and the most nuanced of hints would be well understood at the other end of the communication.

I have remembered this many times when I have read or preached on the book of Revelation. Strange monsters abound, terrible creatures loom up from nowhere, and words and numbers are all wielded in a way that would be familiar to the listener or reader but less so to any on the outside. The readings to which we now turn begin with some of the greatest hymns ever written, which give voice to the great triumph of the cross and resurrection. They capture the apostolic conviction that these two events are pivotal for all time and eternity, and it is by his life laid down that Jesus has set his people free. The great triumph of the lamb heralds, however, a violent response from the powers and principalities, whose lack of accountability and whose resolve to do much as they please propel them further into misery and the judgement of God.

Our readings are now thought to be best understood not so much as a sequence of events predicting the future so much as repeating oracles which describe the age-old struggle between God and the forces of evil. Readers are encouraged to read between the extracts to get the full picture. As each chapter begins with heaven's praise and ends with such powerful warnings, the themes of response and repentance are paramount. If we are ultimately accountable for our choices, we are also responsible for turning and discovering the light and life promised in Jesus. These themes are not unique to Revelation, but they have a force, urgency and power which make them as compelling today as when they were first written.

ANDY JOHN

Who is worthy?

I saw a mighty angel proclaiming with a loud voice, 'Who is worthy to open the scroll and break its seals?'… And I began to weep bitterly because no one was found worthy to open the scroll or to look into it. Then one of the elders said to me, 'Do not weep. See, the Lion of the tribe of Judah, the Root of David, has conquered, so that he can open the scroll and its seven seals.'

In these opening verses we are introduced to one of the author's most important themes: the supreme worthiness of Jesus. This passage points to one of the key questions in the New Testament: how can fallen human beings stand before a perfect and holy God? Wonderfully, the focus is not upon the problem but God's solution.

The picture shows God on the throne representing ultimate power and authority. Only God holds the knowledge of what is still to come and how human history will unfold. The scrolls are in God's hands alone; they are sealed and their contents disclosable only by royal authority.

The author's grief is inconsolable, because there is no one who can break the seals and open the scrolls. At the moment of greatest despair a voice rings out announcing there is one who can open the seals: the 'Lion of the tribe of Judah' and the 'Root of David' has triumphed. There is no mistaking the force of this vision: Jesus, the one born in the lineage of the great King David has won the right to open the seals. His triumph elevates him above all others. In the language of Paul, this is the one before whom every knee shall bow and every tongue confess (Philippians 2:10). His stature is without equal in heaven and earth.

We will encounter much more of both the problem presented by the scrolls, seals and who can make their contents known, but today the focus rests on the one who can claim the title 'Lord' as no other, Jesus Christ.

You are worthy, Lord Jesus Christ, because you alone have authority to do what no one else could do, and you deserve heaven and earth's deepest praise. Amen

ANDY JOHN

Heaven's Hall of Fame

Then I saw between the throne and the four living creatures and among the elders a Lamb standing as if it had been slaughtered, having seven horns and seven eyes, which are the seven spirits of God sent out into all the earth. He went and took the scroll from the right hand of the one who was seated on the throne. When he had taken the scroll, the four living creatures and the twenty-four elders fell before the Lamb.

Many organisations and causes have a Hall of Fame, where heroes are inducted on the basis of their contribution. Access is by invitation only, and though many might feel deserving, few are chosen.

With the disclosure that there is one whose authority is so great that the seals and scroll may be opened, we are introduced a little more to the one who rightly stands in heaven's Hall of Fame. Standing between the throne of God and among the elders is the victor. But we don't see a gladiator dressed in the champion's robes, nor an emperor in finest linen. We see, rather, a lamb standing as though it had been slaughtered. It is his own death which bestows authority to open the seals. The lamb with seven horns and eyes is the author and pioneer of those who belong to him 'sent out into all the earth'. Uninvited therefore (his own worth is sufficient), the lamb takes the scroll as the elders fall down in adoration.

Our reading locks together the most significant events in history: the cross and resurrection of Jesus. If his worth is revealed by his great triumph (see yesterday's reading), it is his death which establishes it and allows him to disclose the scroll's contents. It is both the cross and the resurrection that bring Jesus the legitimate right to be overseer, lord of all things in heaven and on earth.

Lamb of God, you take away the sins of the world and are worthy,
as no other, to know and order the affairs of this world,
for you alone are Lord. Amen

ANDY JOHN

Worthy is the lamb

Then I looked, and I heard the voice of many angels surrounding the throne and the living creatures and the elders; they numbered myriads of myriads and thousands of thousands, singing with full voice, 'Worthy is the Lamb that was slaughtered to receive power and wealth and wisdom and might and honour and glory and blessing!' Then I heard every creature in heaven and on earth and under the earth and in the sea, and all that is in them, singing, 'To the one seated on the throne and to the Lamb be blessing and honour and glory and might forever and ever!'

The songs of adoration flow from what we now know about this lamb, slaughtered and triumphant, worshipped by every creature in heaven and on earth. The scale of this worship is remarkable, because it includes all living things giving voice to the majesty of God and the lamb.

It was common for the emperor to be worshipped by virtue of inherited status or conquest of other nations. As we read that the lamb also receives adoration, it points to his identity. Who, other than God, is worthy of worship? When we recall that this praise is given to the 'man of sorrows', the babe of Bethlehem, we might well be astonished.

These extraordinary songs hold in tension something which is bold and essential. The lamb is revealed as mortal (he died) but divine (worthy of worship), not identical to the one on the throne but apart from the elders and angels. In these songs a picture is built of one who is truly human and fully divine. Like all true worship, these things are not offered as cold dogma but invitations to faith. When we hear the angelic song, we are summoned to worship with the same vibrancy they bring. This can be a challenge when life is difficult or when there are few of us gathered together. It is then more than ever that we need to hear the angels' song afresh.

You are indeed worthy, Lord Jesus Christ, for you laid down your life and have set your people free. To you be endless praise forever. Amen

ANDY JOHN

White horses and red riders

Then I saw the Lamb open one of the seven seals, and I heard one of the four living creatures call out, as with a voice of thunder, 'Come!' I looked, and there was a white horse!... When he opened the second seal, I heard the second living creature call out, 'Come!' And out came another horse, bright red; its rider was permitted to take peace from the earth.

Our reading today introduces the first two of four riders whose appearance is linked to the opening of the seals. Each brings different kinds of calamity upon earth in a vision which sounds shocking and frightening. Most commentators believe the following visions describe not separate events but underline ongoing themes; the realities described are repeated in different ways to give them force and greater weight.

The first two riders ride out to bring war and disorder. The white horse and rider are bent on conquest, and the second, a fiery red horse, even more alarmingly, to withdraw peace and cause mortals to fight against each other.

The realities to which these visions give rise are tragically familiar and are repeated throughout human history. It is not only the seemingly irresistible appetite for war which characterises human life, but also domination of others. One rider brings conflict, the other the absence of peace. With both, fighting is normalised as people wrestle for supremacy and control.

Although history shows that Christians don't have an unblemished record in matters of conflict, today's message cannot be denied. When powerful forces are unleashed without control, there is ruin. It is therefore essential that we recall that the riders are not operating beyond the reach of God. They remain servants. And as such their purpose is to reveal what a godless landscape looks like. There is both warning and exhortation here: to choose a pathway that resists violence and domination and finds in the example of the lamb and his death all that it promises and requires. It is this which must become our pattern of living.

Sovereign King, extend your rule and reign of peace on earth,
where swords become ploughshares and justice flows like a river,
for Jesus Christ's sake. Amen

ANDY JOHN

Pale and black horses

When [the Lamb] opened the third seal, I heard the third living creature call out, 'Come!' I looked, and there was a black horse! Its rider held a pair of scales in his hand… When he opened the fourth seal, I heard the voice of the fourth living creature call out, 'Come!' I looked and there was a pale green horse! Its rider's name was Death.

Two further horses with their riders are sent out following the breaking of the seals, and both have functions to carry out. The first, the black horse, represents justice, but in a way more foreboding than we might think. The second, the pale green horse, represents death, whom we know is described in the New Testament as the final enemy (1 Corinthians 15:26).

There is no mistaking the notion of judgement in both of these agents loosed by God. The scales of justice show that humanity has fallen short and is found wanting; the second that the grave awaits us all. Death, personified here as a rider, is not only the embodiment of a natural end to human lives but is also seen as a figure who represents separation from God.

As this heavenly drama is worked out, we see patterns: unaccountable humanity is prone to destructive behaviour and the desire to dominate. The analysis from today's reading is that human beings are found wanting and death is the end.

Although these figures are presented to us in vivid, almost theatrical, portrayals, the realities they describe are real and serious. Any critique of the world will need to understand that there are vested interests and powerful motivators which affect and control global decisions, and these are not always benign. Such drivers are all too often the things which, from the beginning, have dominated human destiny, such as greed and wilfulness. And it is these, as much as anything else, from which we must be rescued and saved

---

Judge of all, we see in your servants the very sins which not only control much in our world but to which we are also attached. Save us and help us we pray, in Jesus' name. Amen

ANDY JOHN

Run to the hills

When he opened the sixth seal… there came a great earthquake; the sun became black as sackcloth, the full moon became like blood, and the stars of the sky fell to the earth… Then the kings of the earth and the magnates and the generals and the rich and the powerful, and everyone, slave and free, hid in caves and among the rocks of the mountains, calling to the mountains and rocks, 'Fall on us and hide us from the face of the one seated on the throne and from the wrath of the Lamb; for the great day of their wrath has come, and who is able to stand?'

Following the opening of the last seal we read of the calamity which comes to earth. It reads like something from a modern disaster or sci-fi movie. The scale of the terror is so great that every kind of ruler and government is reduced to abject despair as they plead for their own destruction.

Although this kind of passage can seem frightening, this is not the author's intention. Instead, he is making two crucial points. The first is that these 'powers' which have ruled without accountability are now subject to the judgement of the lamb. We remember the context in which this is written, when powerful authorities wielded their influence uninhibited. It may appear to the naked eye that this is the only reality. In a world which still sees considerable corruption and dreadful abuses, we will understand this point well.

Yet there is another reality to grasp, and it is that the powers are all subject, ultimately, to God and to the lamb. Final sovereign rule lies with God and none other. This conviction would have encouraged the early persecuted Christians enormously, because it strengthened their faith that the world was not meaningless and that events could have purpose, even if that purpose was hidden from them. We can relate to this same challenge today, because there are many who would suggest that the world, indeed the universe, is without meaning. The passage helps us know that we are kept always in the care of our God, and that to work for the transformation of all life is the greatest expression of faith we could offer.

Living God, we know we are held secure in your powerful love. Hasten the coming of your kingdom when justice flows like a river. Amen

ANDY JOHN

One hundred and forty-four thousand

He called with a loud voice to the four angels who had been given power to damage earth and sea, saying, 'Do not damage the earth or the sea or the trees, until we have marked the servants of our God with a seal on their foreheads.' And I heard the number of those who were sealed, one hundred and forty-four thousand, sealed out of every tribe of the people of Israel.

Once more we note that authority resides with God across the whole of creation. Angels, now instruments of God's judgement, are given power to worsen what sounds already to be a terrible situation. The New Testament speaks elsewhere that judgement is revealed by the increase of disobedience and chaos (Romans 1:21–23), so that it is plain what happens when human beings are left to their own devices.

But the angels are also given authority to mark the foreheads of those 'out of every tribe of the people of Israel'. It is likely that you will have received a visit from those commonly known as Jehovah's Witnesses and perhaps been persuaded to engage in a conversation about this text. The idea that there are only 144,000 who will stand before God is not an accurate belief. The significance of the number is that each of the tribes of Israel is included. This is another New Testament 'perfect number', like the 40 days of Jesus' fasting in the wilderness. The material point is these are all included in the family of God because they know Jesus Christ. It is their relationship to him which marks and seals them as God's very own.

Our passage is not meant to be read as a mathematical formula, nor to invite us to ponder on who is included and who is not. It is rather to underline the deep security Christians possess. Their faith is not only a matter of personal choice; God has called and chosen us, and it is this which gives hope that we will neither falter not fail.

Almighty God, you hold all things as sovereign Lord. Strengthen our faith in you even as we face our own challenges which could otherwise overwhelm us. Amen

ANDY JOHN

Echoes of Palm Sunday

After this I looked, and there was a great multitude that no one could count, from every nation, from all tribes and peoples and languages, standing before the throne and before the Lamb, robed in white, with palm branches in their hands. They cried out in a loud voice, saying, 'Salvation belongs to our God who is seated on the throne, and to the Lamb!'

This is not the first time we are presented with a picture of a gathered assembly in heaven giving praise to God. In Revelation 5 we heard of the angels singing their praises, and here the whole family of God joins them in adoration. Yesterday we read that the number of those chosen (the 144,000 perfect number) is representative, signifying the complete total, so that none who belong are on the outside.

Today we see their primary role, which is to give praise to God and to the Lamb. There are two things which are noteworthy here. The first is that they give voice to the great triumph of God over the forces of darkness. Because every foe is defeated and every power laid low, there is only one fitting response, and that is worship. Once, the crowds, perhaps few in number, waved their palms before a man who rode on a donkey; here it is the innumerable number whose hope is in the Word made flesh that do likewise.

The second noteworthy point is that the number of those assembled is drawn from across the whole world. This great assembly has a wondrous variety. Just as the gospel was preached to all the ends of the earth, so from across the continents they are gathered here. But there is perhaps even more to be acknowledged here: this great number is representative of Christ's redeeming work – work that touches all of creation, not just humanity. God's triumph is truly all-encompassing, and it is this which elicits endless praise.

Mighty God and precious Saviour, we join the angels and multitudes in praise of your great victory. As you have triumphed over hell and death, make us abound in hope and to be responsive to your call here and now. For the sake of the lamb who was slain. Amen

ANDY JOHN

The lamb on the throne

Then one of the elders asked me, 'These in white robes – who are they, and where did they come from?' I answered, 'Sir, you know.' And he said... 'They are before the throne of God and serve him day and night in his temple; and he who sits on the throne will shelter them with his presence. "Never again will they hunger; never again will they thirst. The sun will not beat down on them," nor any scorching heat. For the Lamb at the centre of the throne will be their shepherd; "he will lead them to springs of living water." "And God will wipe away every tear from their eyes."'

This dialogue opens up the great hope Christians possess – that our lives are hidden with Christ in God (Colossians 3:3) and all eternity awaits us. Once more the language is rich but needs some unpacking if we are to grasp the breadth of this hope.

Again we remember that the church was facing hostile persecution at this time. The temptation for many Christians was either to avoid public acknowledgement or expression of their faith or to capitulate to external pressure. The letter to the Hebrews is written with this in mind (see Hebrews 12:4 especially), but the situation addressed here appears graver still, and the threat of death very real. Those in white robes are Christians who have survived the persecution, yet the focus is not on their survival but upon the protection afforded them by God. Earthly harm and scorching heat will no longer afflict them, because the lamb will be their shepherd.

As we continue to experience the consequences of the Covid pandemic, one of the questions I have wrestled with as a Christian and a bishop is whether some of the new uncertainty has invited a fresh awareness of some of the heavenly certainties promised by God? This might sound old-fashioned, but at the heart of our faith is a promise of eternal fellowship with God. The early Christians were strengthened in their faith as they held this hope and it sustained them. I find myself challenged afresh by their resolve and encouraged by the word which invites me to trust in the shepherd whose protection is without equal.

Lord Jesus Christ, shepherd of the flock, you have promised to hold us for all eternity. May we trust in you anew this day and beyond. Amen

ANDY JOHN

Silence in heaven

When the Lamb opened the seventh seal, there was silence in heaven for about half an hour… Another angel with a golden censer came and stood at the altar; he was given a great quantity of incense to offer… And the smoke of the incense… rose before God from the hand of the angel. Then the angel took the censer and filled it with fire from the altar and threw it on the earth.

One of the most intriguing incidents in the book of Revelation occurs in this passage: the silence in heaven. We can imagine the silence heralds something significant. But we might be surprised at what follows, because there is no new vanquishing of enemies or fresh crowning of the lamb. Instead, angels mix incense with the prayers of the saints which rise up to God. It is the prayerfulness of the saints and the worship of heaven which is so profound that only silence could accompany it.

While the worship of God stands central to the whole of this book, there are two things which stand out. The first is that the silence elevates this worship to a new level. Whatever else we might prize here on earth, the worship of God is more important still. Our worship encompasses all of our life and is so much more than hymns or songs. It is the content of our whole life.

Second, it is this which is unleashed on the earth. The prayers and adoration of God are more powerful than we can know and more likely to challenge and invite change in human lives than we suppose. As a young Christian, one of the most significant factors in nurturing my faith was the vibrancy of the worship I experienced. Matched with lives that embodied love in action, it was life-changing and helped me make connections between what I read in the scriptures and what I experienced in my daily life. Today's passage is an invitation to a worship which reflects the joy and triumph of heaven.

Living God, to worship you is to not only honour you but also experience the very thing we were created to offer. May our worship be worthy of all you have given to us. Amen

ANDY JOHN

Woe and calamity

The fourth angel blew his trumpet, and a third of the sun was struck, and a third of the moon, and a third of the stars, so that a third of their light was darkened; a third of the day was kept from shining, and likewise the night. Then I looked, and I heard an eagle crying with a loud voice as it flew in mid-heaven, 'Woe, woe, woe to the inhabitants of the earth, at the blasts of the other trumpets that the three angels are about to blow!'

Following yesterday's reading, angels are once more engaged in bringing about the will of God. Previously, they extolled the perseverance of the saints and the saving protection of God. Here, they are instruments of woe. The entire passage encapsulates all of creation – the earth, sea, rivers and sky – which bears the consequences of humanity's ills. Once more this is a terrifying picture lacking faith and hope.

It would be easy for us to despair at the images employed here and, regarding the visions as predictions of what is to come, become more despondent. We have seen already, however, that these visions are not successive events so much as oracles which describe ongoing realities. Their power lies in what they reveal about God and humanity. Also, they are unremitting in their assessment: humanity is under judgement for departing from the truth. God holds people to account and will not be indifferent nor impotent to act in the face of wrongdoing and injustice.

Paul was equally emphatic in his letter to the Romans: 'But by your hard and impenitent heart you are storing up wrath for yourself on the day of wrath' (Romans 2:5). It is interesting that the apostle also saw that God's kindness is meant to lead us to repentance (Romans 2:4). These two qualities are always held together in God, and as one holds us accountable for sin, so the other invites a response to his grace. We need both to follow the Lord.

Lord God, help us to live lives which hold together the values we see in you and are enabled to embrace through your Holy Spirit. Amen

ANDY JOHN

Locusts and scorpions

Then from the smoke came locusts on the earth, and they were given authority like the authority of scorpions of the earth. They were told not to damage the grass of the earth or any green growth or any tree, but only those people who do not have the seal of God on their foreheads. They were allowed to torture them for five months, but not to kill them, and their torture was like the torture of a scorpion when it stings someone. And in those days people will seek death but will not find it; they will long to die, but death will flee from them.

The fifth angel opens up the great pit from which all manner of horrors are released: there are locusts who have the ability to sting like a scorpion, and even though people will long for death, it will evade them. This particular judgement is reserved for those who do not have the seal of God on their foreheads.

These striking and vivid chapters introduce a further dimension to the theme of judgement. The most striking element is that death, often regarded as an unwelcome intrusion on and curtailment to life, is denied those who lack God's favour. The meaning is unmistakable: the torment to come is so great that even death would be a release. This release is denied to those who are outside the household of faith.

One of the great themes of scripture is that wickedness is not only perilous but is ultimately self-defeating. Acts of rebellion might promise a great deal at the time, but as the story of Adam and Eve's disobedience reveals, there is only heartache to follow (Genesis 3:10ff). Here we see the same theme: instead of enduring bliss, there is the fruit of agony and pain which follows rebellion. We are not only brought near to the terrible reality which follows disobedience but also shown how pitifully pointless such rebellion is. Sometimes the sheer force of what seems to be negative is necessary for the problem to be properly recognised. This is undoubtedly the case in today's reading.

Lord God, as we understand the pitfalls of walking away from you, give us a constant stream of grace and wisdom to walk closely at your side each day. In Christ's name. Amen

ANDY JOHN

Abaddon and Apollyon

They had scales like iron breastplates, and the noise of their wings was like the noise of many chariots with horses rushing into battle. They have tails like scorpions, with stings, and in their tails is their power to harm people for five months. They have as king over them the angel of the bottomless pit; his name in Hebrew is Abaddon, and in Greek he is called Apollyon.

This vision of locusts is as grotesque as any which we might find in the scriptures, and deliberately so. The visualisation of what is truly terrible is a powerful piece of rhetoric, which states plainly what the nature of the antichrist looks like. Again the vision would be at home in a Hollywood film, yet this is no fantasy but rather an exposé of life bereft of accountability and godliness.

The writer locates the source of this hoard's authority in the king from the pit, the angel of Abaddon. This term is used on six occasions in the Bible and is closely associated with Sheol, the place of the dead. But here the authority is wielded with new force because the king and his hoards are very much alive and bent on destruction. Woven into the narrative of the book and yet more powerful is a deep understanding that sin and godless-ness have a spiritual character. The manifestation of this can be physical, structural and personal, but at the root of the malaise there is something both profoundly spiritual and malevolent.

Too often we minimise the scale and horror of evil by imagining every mishap is the work of the devil. Yet it is not difficult to see what happens when power is unleashed without any accountability or restraint. When people are crushed and the earth despoiled and there is no shame, such things take on a hellish character that seems to be all of a piece with what we read here. The painfully obvious conclusion is that such forces must be taken seriously.

Almighty God, teach us never to fear evil but to unmask the powers that are at variance with your kingdom. Help us long for righteousness and the coming of your reign. In Jesus Christ. Amen

ANDY JOHN

Idols and alternatives

By these three plagues a third of humankind was killed... For the power of the horses is in their mouths and in their tails... The rest of humankind, who were not killed by these plagues, did not repent of the works of their hands or give up worshipping demons and idols of gold and silver and bronze and stone and wood, which cannot see or hear or walk. And they did not repent.

Our final reading ends with an unfolding catastrophe of unrestrained violence and war. It is a staggering vision of destruction and death on a scale which must have alarmed the early readers of this work. Those who have witnessed or chronicled genocides and the scale of slaughter in successive world wars will read these words with grim solemnity rather than disbelief.

Yet the writer offers a perspective which lies at the heart of the biblical revelation (Exodus 7:20ff), that the purpose of judgement is to turn the hearts of people back to God. This underscores what we have seen consistently, which is that God holds human beings accountable for their deeds and omissions. There is a dignity but responsibility to be apprehended here: although we are undoubtedly the product of genes and shaped inevitably by our social surroundings, we are capable of exercising decision-making powers. For this reason, wonderfully and fearfully made as we are (Psalm 139:14), we have a freedom both in the way we act and in the capacity to turn from what is wrong and to do good.

The painful conclusion the writer draws at the end of the chapter is that despite the severe penalties exacted, human beings did not repent or turn back to God. In what sounds like a despairing conclusion, we might hear an echo of God searching for Adam in the garden (Genesis 3:9); of the angel wrestling with Jacob (Genesis 32:22ff); possibly also of Christ dying on the cross (Luke 23:34).

Living God, you call us to walk with you humbly and to reject what is evil. Turn our hearts from every kind of wrong and enable us to choose what is right in the sight of your Son, Jesus Christ. Amen

ANDY JOHN

Psalms 40—51

For the next fortnight, we are going to ponder a selection of psalms.

The psalms take us from one extreme of human emotion to another: from joy to sadness; from despair to hope; from doubt to trust; from death to life, with may gradations in between, often even in one psalm.

The psalms come from many different backgrounds, in different centuries of the history of God's people. Although often referred to as the psalms of David, they don't all belong to his time. For example, Psalm 74 refers to the destruction of the temple, and Psalm 137 describes the people in exile by the waters of Babylon, events which occurred long after David's reign. There are also several authors and musicians named alongside some of the psalms, suggesting that this way of expressing their response to events was commonplace.

The psalms take us to our feelings. Some are expressions of thanksgiving. We usually don't find it hard to express our joy and delight when life is good. Where we find more difficulty is in expressing our feelings when life is a struggle or, worse, falls apart. Often, we think we shouldn't feel the way we do. But the psalms help us to understand that we can be completely honest with God. We don't have to pretend; God knows exactly how we think and feel, and nothing about us will stop God loving us.

There are some fairly brutal passages in the psalms, and people are sometimes tempted to leave them out. It is probably appropriate to leave out these 'cursing' verses during public worship, because it might give a wrong impression about the kind of God we worship to someone who has just dropped in to see what is going on. But we need to learn that in our personal moments with God, what God wants is honesty. If we pretend that we never have negative or violent thoughts, we will never change. We don't shock God by being honest, but we do open ourselves up to being changed, and that's the way to becoming whole.

ANN LEWIN

The importance of waiting

I waited patiently for the Lord; he inclined to me and heard my cry. He drew me up from the desolate pit, out of the miry bog, and set my feet upon a rock, making my steps secure. He put a new song in my mouth, a song of praise to our God. Many will see it and fear, and put their trust in the Lord.

Waiting is part of life, but it is increasingly countercultural. We live in a world where things have to be done now. Emails and phones give us instant communication. Next-day delivery offers instant gratification of our material wants. As a result of being part of a global supply chain, we have lost sight of the annual agricultural cycle, so we eat food out of season.

But we know that life itself is the result of waiting. Those nine months in the womb for humans can't be hurried. If for any reason they are interrupted, either a life is lost or premature birth puts normal growth at risk.

Realising that it was the warmth of the sun that enabled it to develop into a butterfly, a scientist once applied some heat to a chrysalis, and watched with delight as a butterfly emerged. But the delight turned to horror as the creature's wings crumpled and it died. Attempting to speed up the natural process had prevented the creature from developing in the proper way.

Spiritually, we all need time to grow in our relationship with God. We get impatient with circumstances. Throughout the Covid pandemic, many of us may have wondered, 'How long is this going to go on?' We get impatient with God, just as the psalmist did at times, when God doesn't appear to be doing anything. We get impatient with ourselves, as our growth to holiness doesn't progress very quickly.

If we take time to wait with God, tune in to his time, then God will have a chance to grow his wholeness in us and give us cause to sing a new song.

My soul waits for you in stillness, Lord.
Fill me with your Spirit of praise and joy. Amen

ANN LEWIN

It is God's judgement that matters

Happy are those who consider the poor; the Lord delivers them in the day of trouble. The Lord protects them and keeps them alive... As for me, I said, 'O Lord, be gracious to me; heal me, for I have sinned against you'... All who hate me whisper together about me; they imagine the worst for me... But you have upheld me because of my integrity, and set me in your presence forever.

It is not always easy when we read Psalms to work out who is being spoken about. In this psalm, the writer begins by describing the blessing given to those who consider the poor. Or he may be describing the blessings God gives the poor when they are cared for. Or he may be reminding us that the poor and needy can be a blessing to us. God surprises us into fresh understanding in many ways. I once gave some food and drink to a young homeless man, sitting wrapped in his duvet in the cold, and he replied, 'God bless you' – and I thought I was the one giving the blessing.

The psalmist then goes on to ask for mercy for himself, for he feels that he needs to be healed because of his sin. He is the victim of a whispering campaign against him: his enemies wish for his death, and even his closest friend has betrayed him.

The psalm changes direction again, and the writer thanks God that he has not let his enemies win but has recognised his integrity and accepted him into his presence. The psalmist ends by blessing God for his faithfulness.

It seems that after being cast down over what people are saying about him, and the sense of betrayal he feels, the writer decides that what other people think about him and the way they treat him are not as important as what God believes about him. When we find ourselves feeling that everyone is against us, we need to remember that we are profoundly loved and that nothing we do will make God change his mind about our value.

Lord, fill us with hope when our hearts are heavy and we feel unloved. Renew our trust in your faithfulness. Amen

ANN LEWIN

Longing for God

As the deer longs for flowing streams, so my soul longs for you, O God. My soul thirsts for God, for the living God. When shall I come and behold the face of God? My tears have been my food day and night, while people say to me continually, 'Where is your God?'

'I'll tell you what I want, what I really really want,' sang the Spice Girls in 1996. The song stayed in the charts for a long time, presumably because it echoed a restlessness in people's hearts, a dissatisfaction with life as it had to be lived at the time. Many people would have answered in material terms, for the 'must have things', like a house they could afford or secure employment. Others would have wanted emotional satisfaction through better relationships or a rewarding job.

In spiritual terms, Augustine of Hippo, in the fourth century, put the Christian longing in words that have become familiar over the centuries: 'God, you have made us for yourself, and our hearts are restless till they find their rest in you.'

That is the thirst our psalmist speaks of today, thirst for a deeper relationship with God. Spending time with God; pondering the scriptures; listening when we pray – all these will help us to go deeper. That relationship is always a gift from God, not something we achieve by trying harder.

In the 17th century, Brother Lawrence, in addition to attending services in chapel, practised the presence of God in the busy kitchen of the monastery where he lived. When asked how he did it, he said that whenever he was not actively engaged in cooking, he turned his attention to God, with the result that he felt he 'possessed God in as great tranquillity as when he was on his knees at the Blessed Sacrament'. That would not have happened overnight; going deeper is a life-long journey. But what a reward awaits us if we set out on it.

In the 14th century, Julian of Norwich gave us words we can use as a prayer: 'God, of your goodness give us yourself, for if we ask for anything which is less we shall always be in want; only in you we have all.' Amen

ANN LEWIN

Feeling abandoned

Why have you cast me off? Why must I walk about mournfully because of the oppression of the enemy? O send out your light and truth, let them lead me; let them bring me to your holy hill and to your dwelling. Then I will go to the altar of God, to God my exceeding joy; and I will praise you with the harp, O God, my God… Hope in God, for I shall again praise him, my help and my God.

The psalms sometimes move quite quickly from expressing confidence in God to complaining about apparent abandonment. We don't know what provoked this particular outburst: it could have been any one of the many challenges the Hebrew people were faced with during their long history.

On the other hand the enemy may not have been an external force at all. Sometimes the enemy lies within, an expression of our 'glass half-empty' – or in some cases completely empty – attitude to life. It is very easy when we feel overwhelmed by whatever is challenging us to feel that there is nothing worth living for. During the worst times of the Covid pandemic, people were encouraged to put a symbol of a rainbow in their windows in support for the NHS. They were also a reminder that God had once put a rainbow in the sky as a sign of hope for the future.

Deep down, the psalmist knew where the answer to his feeling of distress would come from. Although he felt abandoned, he knew that God's light and truth could bring him out of his pit of depression or self-pity or whatever was getting to him, and bring him to a state where he could again worship and praise God. He told himself, as he had done at the end of Psalm 42, to hope and trust in God, who is the one who can help.

Like learning to practise the presence of God, learning to trust God is an act of will. Our prayer may not make any difference to our outward circumstances, but it will change our mindset and strengthen our hope.

Lord, when we feel abandoned and helpless,
strengthen us to hope and trust in you. Amen

ANN LEWIN

The place of lamentation

We have heard with our ears, O God, our ancestors have told us, what deeds you performed in their days… In God we have boasted continually, and we will give thanks to your name forever. Yet you have rejected us and abased us, and have not gone out with our armies… All this has come upon us, yet we have not forgotten you, or been false to your covenant… Rouse yourself! Why do you sleep, O Lord?… Rise up, come to our help. Redeem us for the sake of your steadfast love.

This psalm is an example of the plain-speaking dialogue which pervades the whole collection of psalms. The writer begins by recalling all the wonderful things he has heard about God's dealings with his people. But their present experience is of one of rejection. God has not gone out with their army, they have been defeated in battle, and they are a laughingstock in the sight of their enemies. They have not been disloyal to God, so why has God deserted them? The psalmist's disappointment leads him to be sharp with God: 'Wake up, and deliver us.'

Lament is a very important aspect of our spiritual life. It is an honest expression of our feelings of hurt, betrayal, abandonment or frustration. We can sometimes feel that we should not be feeling angry: we may have been taught as children that anger was not acceptable. These outbursts in the psalms demonstrate to us that we can be honest with God. God knows what we are feeling anyway, but we need to acknowledge our anger or despair, so that we can move on, rather than letting our negativity fester inwardly.

Lament is not whinging or moaning, but rather telling it as it is, calling a halt to the inner churning which gets us nowhere. The psalmist lets us complain, but he counters the complaint with a statement of faith in the God who will never let us down. When we do that, we can begin to move on, get things in perspective and remember again how God has been faithful in his love, even when our fellow human beings have treated us badly.

When we feel that you are absent, Lord, come to us and strengthen us to take hold of our life again. Amen

ANN LEWIN

The importance of celebration

You are the most handsome of men; grace is poured upon your lips; therefore God has blessed you forever... Therefore God, your God, has anointed you with the oil of gladness beyond your companions; your robes are all fragrant with myrrh and aloes and cassia. From ivory palaces stringed instruments make you glad; daughters of kings are among your ladies of honour, at your right hand stands the queen in gold of Ophir... The princess is decked in her chamber with gold-woven robes; in many coloured robes she is led to the king.

Whatever calamities the Jewish people endured, they certainly knew how to celebrate a wedding. We don't know which royal wedding this psalm refers to, but obviously no expense was spared and the pageantry was impressive. The language used to describe the event is evocative of the sounds and scents of a great occasion. It is good to know that as well as agonising over difficulties and struggling to survive when faced with strong enemies, God's people would take time to celebrate.

The Covid pandemic led to a hiatus of public celebrations. In family circles, weddings and baptisms were often postponed, while funerals were held with only a few people able to attend. Large gatherings were forbidden for months at a time, sports events were cancelled, and even Christmas limited to small family gatherings.

As well as the fun of gathering together, celebrations mark important occasions. Another aspect of those Covid years was the experience of students at all levels who got to the end of their courses without having a ceremony to mark the occasion. It was a real experience of deprivation at a significant moment in their lives. As life gradually opened up again, people were glad to be able to enjoy celebrations again, and many people took the first opportunity they could to gather together to mark important occasions that had occurred during the time of restrictions.

Lord, help us to keep hope alive and to celebrate
the good things in life. Amen

ANN LEWIN

Do not be afraid

God is our refuge and strength, a very present help in trouble. Therefore we will not fear, though the earth should change, though the mountains shake in the heart of the sea; though its waters roar and foam, though the mountains tremble with its tumult… 'Be still, and know that I am God! I am exalted among the nations, I am exalted in the earth.' The Lord of hosts is with us; the God of Jacob is our refuge.

'God is our refuge and strength… therefore we will not fear.' But the truth is that we have been very afraid for the past couple of years. Quite apart from any personal challenges we may have had, the earth and the sea have been in danger of losing their boundaries. Wildfires, volcanic eruptions and floods have destroyed homes and livelihoods. Rising sea levels have meant that whole communities in some of the remote islands in the Pacific Ocean have had to relocate to the nearest mainland.

The Covid pandemic has taken away many of the certainties we took for granted: loved ones have died, families have been ripped apart and the NHS, on which we relied to keep us healthy, has been stretched to the limit. People's lives and livelihoods have been destroyed. Children's development in educational and social skills have been stunted. It is not surprising that we have been afraid.

But we must not let fear paralyse us. We need to dig deep into our faith and let our fear fuel action to make our world a better place. Acting out of fear can lead to panic, but the psalmist encourages us to replace fear with trust: 'Be still, and know that I am God!' Look around and see the evidence that God cares for his creation, and be reassured that God is with us, whatever life throws at us. We can work with God to reach out with compassion and understanding to people who are afraid, and encourage them to join us in building a better future.

Lord of all life, when we are at our wits end and hope seems lost, come to us and strengthen us to work for the common good. Amen

ANN LEWIN

Praise God

Clap your hands, all you peoples; shout to God with loud songs of joy. For the Lord, the Most High, is awesome, a great king over all the earth... Sing praises to God, sing praises; sing praises to our King, sing praises. For God is the king of all the earth, sing praises with a psalm. God is king over the nations; God sits on his holy throne.

In this psalm, human beings, as representatives of the whole of creation, are called to praise our great and wonderful God. It is a wonderfully exuberant psalm, but we can't help being aware of the other side of the story. In some places people are oppressed by tyrannical regimes. People are starving, suffering from many diseases, weighed down by injustice. All these factors inhibit people from praising God.

The natural world also finds it hard to respond to God with joy when it is being abused and exploited by people with vested interests or those who are irresponsible in their use of the resources we are meant to steward and share. The natural world is in danger of losing its resilience, as a whole range of creatures is driven to the edge of extinction.

We can easily be overwhelmed by the relentless recitation of statistics, and in the light of our recent experience of the pandemic be driven to despair. There is so much to do, and many individuals feel that the little they can do will not make much difference. But we are people of hope, and one thing we can all do is try to help people think less about what we might lose and think more about what we might do to save the planet because we love it.

Hope is not wishful thinking; it is rooted deeply in the promise God has made over and over again in the history of humanity that he will not leave us to our own devices. So we are called to keep the thread of praise alive as we work for a better, more just world on behalf of the whole of creation.

Praise God from whom all blessings flow.
Praise him, all creatures here below.
Praise him above, ye heavenly host.
Praise Father, Son and Holy Ghost.
(Thomas Ken, 1637–1711)

ANN LEWIN

Building worship

Great is the Lord and greatly to be praised in the city of our God… Within its citadels God has shown himself a sure defence. Then the kings assembled, they came on together. As soon as they saw it, they were astounded; they were in panic, they took to flight… We ponder your steadfast love, O God, in the midst of your temple… this is God, our God forever and ever. He will be our guide forever.

This psalm is a celebration of victory in a battle that was never fought. The enemy took flight as soon as they saw the fortifications of Jerusalem. We don't know which of the many battles in Jewish history this was, but the outcome caused great rejoicing, focused on the temple, which symbolised God's presence, reinforcing their belief that God would never leave them.

There is danger in investing so much in a building that it becomes more important than the truth it was established to enshrine. In contemporary Jewish imagination, Jerusalem was an enormous city and its fortifications substantial. In fact, neither of these things were true, and throughout their history, prophets had warned the people that having the temple was not enough. What God was interested in was not the building and the rituals that were celebrated in it, but people's commitment to living in obedience to his laws. The prophets' warnings were never taken seriously, but there are many psalms which demonstrate the joy people took in going to the temple.

We are having to learn the same lessons today. Reorganisation of resources has confronted us with the need to close some church buildings and to share or repurpose others. It can be very painful for people who have cared for a building, perhaps for many generations, to accept these decisions. Yet the church does not close when a building is no longer in use. The church is the people of God, meeting together for worship and service in their local community. Worship is not only the praise we offer to God, but its outworking for justice and fairness in the world.

Lord, help us to let go of things we can no longer sustain. Fill us with your Spirit of renewal, transforming us and the societies in which we live. Amen

ANN LEWIN

Where shall wisdom be found?

Hear this, all you peoples; give ear, all the inhabitants of the world, both low and high, rich and poor together. My mouth shall speak wisdom; the meditation of my heart shall be understanding. I will incline my ear to a proverb; I will solve my riddle to the music of the harp.

What do we mean by 'wisdom'? It is not the same as knowledge or inform-ation, though both are involved. Perhaps wisdom is more about how we use the information we have. As the well-known saying goes, a knowledgeable person will know that a tomato is a fruit; a wise person will know that it does not go down well in a fruit salad.

We could say that wisdom is what helps us to live well in relationship with God and the rest of the created world. It is the result of insights devel-oped over the years. We are not born with a set of instructions attached, like a pack of self-assembly furniture. We have to grow into ourselves, physically, emotionally and spiritually. Wisdom is not a destination we reach, it is a path we follow. In scripture, wisdom is sometimes personified as a companion on the journey who influences us so profoundly that if we pay attention, we become its embodiment.

How do we get wisdom? Some of it we inherit: timeless wisdom recorded in the proverbs we likely learnt as children, such as 'A stitch in time, saves nine.' Other kinds of wisdom we acquire through experience.

Wisdom lies in the ability to look beyond immediate gratification and go deeper into the meaning of what it is to be human. Jesus kept on encour-aging people to do that when he challenged some of the 'received wis-dom' that people brought from the past, and he offered a new way. 'You have heard that it was said… but I say to you…' was a common refrain used by Jesus.

We are faced with that kind of challenge now as we look to rebuild our lives after the pandemic years and work to save the planet from destruction.

'Lord, help us to accept the things we cannot change, the courage to change the things we can and the wisdom to know the difference. Amen'
(Reinhold Niebuhr, 1892–1971)

ANN LEWIN

The root of all evil?

Do not be afraid when some become rich, when the wealth of their houses increases. For when they die they will carry nothing away; their wealth will not go down after them. Though in their lifetime they count themselves happy – for you are praised when you do well for yourself – they will go to the company of their ancestors who will never again see the light.

'Money is the root of all evil,' sang the Andrews Sisters in 1945. 'Take it away, take it away, take it away.' They were misquoting, of course, as many people do, what Paul wrote to Timothy: 'the love of money is a root of all kinds of evil' (1 Timothy 6:10). But their song went on to say that they had all they needed: 'The one I love, moon and stars above, youth and health, what do I want with wealth?' They recognised that lasting riches lie in our relationships with people who love us and a recognition of the beauty of the natural world around.

We do need money, inevitably. Wealth may present people with many problems, not least of which is knowing how to use the power that goes with it, but a lack of it presents even more difficulties, as all the powerless people in the world would testify. Poverty brings with it hunger, homelessness and the possibility of abuse through slavery or other forms of exploitation. What we need is enough, so that we and our fellow humans can flourish.

In *David Copperfield*, Mr Micawber put it well when he said, 'Annual income 20 pounds, annual expenditure 19 (pounds) 19 (shillings) and 6 (pence), result, happiness. Annual income 20 pounds, annual expenditure 20 pounds nought and six (pence), result, misery.'

Love of money brings with it the temptation to envy, which can lead to destructive behaviour. Becoming wealthy only brings temporary happiness, as the rich cannot take their wealth with them when they die. The wisdom of which the psalm spoke earlier means being content with what we have, being concerned for the poor and needy, and being thankful for God's everlasting care.

Lord, help us to be content with what we have, and to work for justice for those who have nothing. Amen

ANN LEWIN

79

God's deep desire

'Gather to me my faithful ones, who made a covenant with me by sacrifice!… Do I eat the flesh of bulls, or drink the blood of goats? Offer to God a sacrifice of thanksgiving, and pay your vows to the Most High… Those who bring thanksgiving as their sacrifice honour me; to those who go the right way I will show the salvation of God.'

Throughout the Hebrew scriptures we read of sacrifices being offered as a sign that people who are making decisions to serve God really mean what they are saying. But people's understanding of the nature of sacrifice changed over time. One pivotal example is the sacrifice that did not happen, when Abraham realised that God did not want human sacrifices, and Isaac was spared. Nevertheless, the sacrifice of animals continued.

This psalm indicates another shift in understanding: God is not interested in outward ritual acts for their own sake. They count for nothing unless they are matched with deeper commitment. God longs for us to commit ourselves to him with thanksgiving for God's goodness. That commitment must be lived out in our relationships with other people and the created world. Sacrifices do not satisfy God's hunger: what God longs for is thankful hearts and lives lived with gratitude, not just thank-offerings.

This does not mean being cheerful all the time. We cannot give thanks for everything that happens. Living amid a pandemic will have taught us that, if personal suffering had not already convinced us. But even in the middle of the pandemic we could give thanks for God's care and guidance shown in many ways. We saw the dedication and skill of those working in the health service. We marvelled at the commitment of scientists to finding a vaccine. We experienced the growth of neighbourly care, the effort made by people to care for others, even those they did not know.

The practice of being thankful, of counting our blessings, helps us to get things in perspective and keeps hope alive.

'Thou that hast giv'n so much to me, give one thing more, a grateful heart… Not thankful when it pleaseth me; as though your blessings had spare days, but such a heart whose pulse may be thy praise.'
(George Herbert, 1593–1633)

ANN LEWIN

Penitence

Have mercy on me, O God, according to your steadfast love; according to your abundant mercy, blot out my transgressions. Wash me thoroughly from my iniquity, and cleanse me from my sin… You desire truth in the inward being, therefore teach me wisdom in my secret heart.

Psalm 51 is one of several psalms we call 'penitential'. It is often used in Lent, the period when we are encouraged to examine ourselves through God's eyes to discern where we need to grow. Penitence is one of the technical words used in religious circles, which needs some explanation.

Penitence does not mean wallowing in feeling bad about ourselves: it means recognising and admitting our responsibility for offending against God's law and asking for forgiveness.

Penitence leads to repentance, another technical word we don't always understand. Repentance means turning around, changing our direction, which may bring us into conflict with people who are then challenged by our new attitude. It will not always bring us friends.

Penitence is not the same as feeling guilty. Guilt often springs from things we learnt in childhood, unrelated to sin against God. Usually these were things that adults around us – parents, teachers, clergy – found unacceptable or inconvenient. All the things that 'nice children' do not do. There is little in scripture about being nice, but plenty about the need to be truthful, just and kind.

It can be helpful as we try to see ourselves as God sees us, to sit with scripture and listen to what it is telling us about God's love and mercy. When we see how Jesus related to people and when we listen to what he says, we will find plenty to help us work out where we need to ask for God's help.

The psalmist prays for wisdom so that he will not waste energy worrying about things he is not responsible for but so that he can ask for the forgiveness which will set him free to live differently and in turn help him concentrate on matters where he knows he needs God's abundant love and mercy.

Lord, give us grace to take hold of the forgiveness you offer
when we come to you in penitence. Help us to be thankful
for the freedom forgiveness brings. Amen.

ANN LEWIN

Restoration through forgiveness

**Let me hear of joy and gladness; let the bones you have crushed rejoice...
Create in me a clean heart O God and put a new and right spirit within
me. Do not cast me away from your presence and do not take your holy
spirit from me. Restore to me the joy of your salvation, and sustain in
me a willing spirit.**

Once we acknowledge that we have sinned and ask for forgiveness, God
can begin to grow his new life in us, transforming us into the people God
knows we can become. That is a matter for joy and gratitude – for the deep
knowledge that God has us in his hand. The forgiven life is not something
we can take for granted: the psalmist still feels the need to ask God to
keep renewing his spirit within him. We are set free to live responsibly in
relationship with God, other people and the created world. We are not set
free to do what we like. Forgiveness leads to a change of direction and a
deepening gratitude to God for his mercy.

It is worth thinking about the categories of sinful behaviour we need to
be aware of. We are probably familiar with 'doing the things we ought not
to have done' (sins of *commission*) and leaving undone the things we ought
to have done (sins of *omission*). But there is a third category, too: the sins
of *permission*, the things we know to be wrong that we allow to continue
because we are too afraid or too lazy to confront them. Being courageous
in challenging corporate sin is a vital part of Christian living. These sins are
just as damaging to the well-being of others on our planet as the things we
deliberately engage in.

Once we have brought all these to God, to ask for forgiveness, God will
restore us in his infinite mercy. God will sustain us in willingness to relate
to all that is around us in a new way. For being restored is never just for our
own peace of mind, but for the benefit of the whole of creation.

---

*Lord, fill our hearts with joy and praise, that we may witness
to the wonder of your love. Amen*

ANN LEWIN

Spring

'Nothing is so beautiful as spring,' wrote Gerald Manley Hopkins in his poem of that title. Is it the first green shoots after the bare branches and barren earth? Or is it the growing length of the day, light after so much dark? For gardeners it is an exciting time of activity and anticipation. Hope fills the air. It is a time of new beginnings.

What is your favourite symbol of springtime? Lambs, daffodils, fresh green leaf tips? Spring speaks of new life and resurrection. Any metaphor worth its mettle, however, must point to the reality beyond it, and for Christians that is the bodily resurrection of the Lord Jesus himself. Here lies the true source of new life and hope for all creation. Christ's resurrection burst into the world with a newness never seen before. It changed everything. It was real, concrete and powerful.

While it is especially at Easter that we celebrate this moment in history when Christ burst from the tomb and death was defeated, new life and hope may come at any time. In the same way that there is the literal spring growth that transforms the northern hemisphere with freshness, there is a metaphorical spring, too, that can happen in the human heart, which is not limited to the time of year.

Winter, which has its own beauty and lessons to teach us, is apt to stamp on our urge to create. It can be winter in the human soul. Spring reminds us of God's endless creativity. It may have an official start in the calendar, but in reality it tends to be unpredictable – here one day only seemingly to go back underground the next. But it will come, and seeds will emerge when the conditions are right. It is the same with us. Who knows what harvest will come from God's unstoppable power to bring life out of death and transform the deadening cords that bind and hold us in perpetual winter?

Spring growth comes from factors both external, such as light and warm soil, and internal, the DNA that propels life to emerge from the changing seed. As Psalm 139 puts it: 'For it was you who formed my inward parts; you knit me together in my mother's womb… Your eyes beheld my unformed substance' (vv. 13, 16a, NRSV).

LIZ HOARE

An invitation

My beloved speaks and says to me: 'Arise, my love, my fair one, and come away; for now the winter is past, the rain is over and gone. The flowers appear on the earth; the time of singing has come, and the voice of the turtle-dove is heard in our land. The fig tree puts forth its figs, and the vines are in blossom; they give forth fragrance. Arise, my love, my fair one, and come away.'

Song of Songs is a beautiful love song that has challenged interpreters in every century. Does it speak solely of human love? Is it an allegory of something else? Or is it both what it seems to be at face value and an invitation to look deeper into God's ways with us? It is full of sensual imagery: sights, sounds, smells, touch and taste.

In these verses, near the beginning of the poem, the woman is recounting her lover's invitation to get up and go out with him into the dawn to witness the changing season. There is an air of excitement. It is clearly springtime in the land, for all the signs are there: flowers appearing on the ground, birdsong in the air. She is being given an invitation to cast off winter and do something new. She may be shy or timid and need encouragement to get up and go out, and drawing attention to the signs of spring may be her lover's way of trying to provide the encouragement she needs.

Spring is often seen as a time for setting aside old and tired ways and finding energy and vision for something new. A spring clean may be called for. God's invitation to us is always to draw us into new life, yet we so often hang back. It may be fear or a loss of imagination to believe that things could be different. The spring imagery in the Song of Songs urges us to believe that winter need not have the last word. God's love invites us to reconnect with our deepest desires and step out in hope and trust. The earth of our soul may be 'hard as iron', as Christina Rossetti's Christmas poem puts it, but the warmth and light of God's loving gaze is far stronger.

Go outside and look and listen for signs of spring in unlikely places.
Dear Lord, help me to hear your invitation to new life today. Amen

LIZ HOARE

God's timing

For everything there is a season, and a time for every matter under heaven: a time to be born, and a time to die; a time to plant, and a time to pluck up what is planted; a time to kill, and a time to heal; a time to break down, and a time to build up; a time to weep, and a time to laugh; a time to mourn, and a time to dance.

Hopefully the theme of spring coming, particularly if that is your reality right now, will encourage us to seek fresh growth in our walk with God. Yet it is not always the case that our spirits or our circumstances line up with what is going on around us. Like Song of Songs which follows it, the book of Ecclesiastes belongs to what is known as the wisdom literature of the Old Testament. So, what is it saying to us about life and living it well in these few lines?

Ecclesiastes contains the seemingly fatalistic words, 'Vanity of vanities! All is vanity' (1:2), yet here it seems that the author is sure that everything has its time and is as it should be. The writer is concerned that we become wise by living according to God's commandments (12:13). Each season in the natural world has its own rhythm and special features. One of the ways we may grow spiritually is by recovering the natural rhythms of the seasons which many people have almost ceased to notice because we are so insulated by artificial light and central heating.

We are blessed in many parts of the world with clear distinctions between the four seasons. In the northern hemisphere, for gardeners, spring is a time to prepare the ground and plant the seeds. It would be pointless to look for a harvest of apples in spring, because it is not the time for them. There is a time to hunker down and wait, cooperating with nature rather than trying to fight it, trusting that there are unseen things going on. There are times of waiting in the spiritual realm too: learning to trust that God is present and that there are still things going on deep in our hearts through the Spirit's work, even though they might not be obvious.

Lord, my times are in your hands. Thank you for the daily rhythm of life. Help me to trust you each day and in every season. Amen

LIZ HOARE

A new creation

'Very truly I tell you, unless a grain of wheat falls into the earth and dies, it remains just a single grain; but if it dies it bears much fruit. Those who love their life lose it, and those who hate their life in this world will keep it for eternal life. Whoever serves me must follow me, and where I am, there will my servant be also. Whoever serves me, the Father will honour.'

There is a paradox in spring, because for new life to come about there has to be the ending of the old. Winter dominates for so long, but as the days begin to lengthen and the soil warms, the seeds at last have a chance to grow. But what emerges from the earth will not be the same as what went in.

Jesus taught his disciples that unless a grain of wheat falls into the ground and dies it remains a seed. No new life can come out of a seed unless it becomes something else. Dying to self seems so drastic, so counter-intuitive, and yet it is the gateway to fruitfulness and freedom. Christian history is full of stories of people who have discovered the joyous truth of this. The seed has to be transformed to produce the new plant that will bear fruit. It is a hard message to swallow and yet millions have testified to the liberating truth of letting go of self and discovering life in abundance. From famous examples to unknown saints in every age who would not claim to have given up anything, the church has been fruitful because of those who put the Lord Jesus first.

We who profess to follow Christ are not on a journey of self-fulfillment nor one of comfortable ease. The paradox of the Christian life is that in letting go of self, we find our true selves in Christ our Lord. We discover the truth of Paul's testimony that if anyone is in Christ, they are a 'new creation' (2 Corinthians 5:17). The old may have passed away, but that makes way for the new to come. The new that is so full of potential is to be a blessing to the world as we give it away. That little seed has so much to give, and in dying, a fresh harvest of abundance is made possible.

As winter gives way to spring, what in your life do you need to let go of in order for new life to blossom and grow to fruition?

LIZ HOARE

Deep roots

I pray that, according to the riches of his glory, he may grant that you may be strengthened in your inner being with power through his Spirit, and that Christ may dwell in your hearts through faith, as you are being rooted and grounded in love. I pray that you may have the power to comprehend, with all the saints, what is the breadth and length and height and depth, and to know the love of Christ that surpasses knowledge, so that you may be filled with all the fullness of God.

Yesterday's reading looked at the new life that emerges from the seed. Roots are as important as what can be seen emerging above ground. While we look for growth above ground as evidence of healthy life, seeds have to put roots downwards into the soil in order to thrive. In his letter to the Ephesians, Paul writes about God's eternal purpose that he has carried out in Christ Jesus (3:11), and he utters this beautiful prayer of his longing for them. It is a lesson in spiritual growth towards maturity, and it begins with being rooted in God.

What are roots for? They anchor the plant and stop it from being blown or washed away by inclement weather. Indeed, some trees that endure stormy weather patterns have the deepest roots of all. Equally important, roots draw up nourishment and moisture that feed the plant and provide the necessary nutrients for consistent growth.

There are trees that, if you could take a cross-section of them from top to bottom, would show that their roots go as deep and wide beneath the surface as their height and spread of branches are above ground. This natural image echoes Paul's expansive prayer in all its dimensions: breadth and length, height and depth. In the Christian life, such growth comes through the indwelling of Christ through the power of his Holy Spirit. This is how we become rooted and grounded in love, the love of God in Christ that surpasses all human knowledge.

In what ways are you experiencing the need to be rooted and grounded in God's love at this time?

LIZ HOARE

Abiding

Abide in me as I abide in you. Just as the branch cannot bear fruit by itself unless it abides in the vine, neither can you unless you abide in me. I am the vine, you are the branches. Those who abide in me and I in them bear much fruit, because apart from me you can do nothing... My father is glorified by this, that you bear much fruit and become my disciples. As the Father has loved me, so I have loved you; abide in my love.

Anyone who has watched a child asleep in their mother's arms will have some sense of what it means to abide. It conjures up a sense of security, peace, safety and nurture. Jesus looked around him and the image of the branches emerging out of the main vine gave him the metaphor of abiding in God that he wanted his disciples to adopt as their default stance.

For busy 21st-century Christians this is a challenge, because we are not wired to develop the contemplative awareness that learning to abide requires. Abiding seems almost too passive, devoid of activity and the progress we are geared to pursue. But Jesus is very clear that we cannot bear fruit unless we have learned to abide in him. He is the vine, the source of life and nourishment, and without him as our core, we will wither.

Lent offers fresh possibilities in this whole realm by inviting us to pause and pay attention to our spiritual well-being. It is unhelpful to see Lent as yet another time to achieve something. Setting time aside to prepare for Easter by learning again what it means to abide in Jesus could simply mean learning to let go of self-designated goals and achievements.

Jesus assures us in this passage that if we abide in him, we will bear much fruit, and that as a result, his Father in heaven is glorified. As with yesterday's reading about deep-rootedness, the activity that goes on in the hidden depths of our being is God's work. There is an emerging life from within that is not of our own making.

What helps you to abide consciously in God
so that you know you are held securely?

LIZ HOARE

The planting of the Lord

The spirit of the Lord God is upon me, because the Lord has anointed me; he has sent me to bring good news to the oppressed, to bind up the broken-hearted, to proclaim liberty to the captives, and release to the prisoners; to proclaim the year of the Lord's favour, and the day of vengeance of our God; to comfort all who mourn… They will be called oaks of righteousness, the planting of the Lord, to display his glory.

Although the prophet Isaiah has harsh judgements to pronounce on God's people, he also speaks words of hope and restoration. Chapter 61 is such a passage, and it is full of new life and resurrection. It shows how God can bring hope and life to seemingly hopeless situations. Its picture of good news for so many sorrowful and desperate situations captures the imagination of the prophet, who sees God's people as oaks of righteousness. It is a vivid tableau of the resurrection of the people of God and was taken up by Jesus himself at the outset of his ministry (Luke 4:16–21).

Isaiah spoke out of the conviction that he was God's messenger and was anointed by God's Spirit to speak with authority. Today is St Patrick's Day, when the church gives thanks for the mission of Patrick to the Irish people in the fifth century. He too felt the Spirit of God upon him, propelling him back to the land where he had previously been held captive in order to tell them about Christ. He was not the first Christian to try to do this, but his imaginative approach to founding Christian communities brought a fresh new spring that bore such fruit that Ireland in the eighth century became known as 'the land of saints and scholars'.

The end of Isaiah 61 is a fitting epitaph to Patrick's ministry and in keeping with our theme: 'For as the earth brings forth its shoots, and as a garden causes what is sown in it to spring up, so the Lord God will cause righteousness and praise to spring up before all the nations' (61:11).

*Pray for situations you know of that are crying out
for hope and restoration today.*

LIZ HOARE

New beginnings

A voice cries out: 'In the wilderness prepare the way of the Lord, make straight in the desert a highway for our God. Every valley shall be lifted up, and every mountain and hill be made low; the uneven ground shall become level, and the rough places a plain. Then the glory of the Lord shall be revealed, and all people shall see it together, for the mouth of the Lord has spoken.'

In 2011 a series of pro-democracy uprisings began in northern Africa and the Middle East which became known as the 'Arab Spring'. The name echoes other revolutions, such as that in Prague in 1968, all of which aimed to bring about social and political change for the better. Tragically the changes that came about were not all for the better, and the initial hopes were to be dashed in the violence and oppression that followed.

This passage from Isaiah gives words of comfort and hope following many words of judgement. The people who heard this message longed for change that would bring them home, renewing their nation and their relationship with God. They were words of life to those who felt the weight of hopelessness grinding them down.

Our world today desperately needs to hear words of life, to imagine these green shoots of hope for a future that looks different from what is the case right now. The good news of the gospel will have special resonance for those who are trapped in a bleak winter of suffering and injustice. As we ponder the green shoots that we see emerging around us in this spring season, how could they lead us to pray for our communities and perhaps lead us to get involved in encouraging those shoots to grow to fruition? What signs of God are there at work in the forgotten parts of our society? What do we need to do to encourage them? We need to be people who notice what is going on and what God is doing and to join in.

Spend some time praying for your own community, asking God to show you where the green shoots of hope are pushing through the darkness and what he wants you to do to encourage them.

LIZ HOARE

The road home

The wilderness and the dry land shall be glad, the desert shall rejoice and blossom; like the crocus it shall blossom abundantly, and rejoice with joy and singing. The glory of Lebanon shall be given to it, the majesty of Carmel and Sharon. They shall see the glory of the Lord, the majesty of our God. Strengthen the weak hands, and make firm the feeble knees. Say to those who are of a fearful heart, 'Be strong, do not fear! Here is your God'.

Many know the stories associated with Mothering Sunday: of girls who entered service in the households of the wealthy embarking on work that was hard and demanding. On one day each year, they were given time off to go home to visit their mothers. It being spring and the time of blossom and spring flowers, they would pick posies along the way to their mothers as a sign of love and affection.

We still give flowers to show love, sympathy or gratitude, for they seem to symbolise comfort while at the same time pointing beyond the moment to a brighter future full of hope. Flowers for a new birth and flowers for loss are both appropriate. Mothers know much about both, for they accompany the full range of human experience in their nurturing.

In today's passage, Isaiah looks into the future when God's people will return to their homeland. He pictures the desert over which the exiles were driven to an alien land now welcoming them home. There is a highway for them to walk on (v. 8), and the people travel in safety and with joy. It is difficult not to picture contemporary scenes of refugees walking long dusty roads away from violence and destruction, hoping against hope that they will reach safety and a future. Such an image seems a long way from girls traversing English pastureland to visit their mothers, but all humans long for home, for safety and for belonging. They seek the road home, whatever that might look like. A road that is safe and crosses a land blossoming with the hope of spring is a real cause for joy and thanksgiving.

Pray for all who long for the love and security of home.

LIZ HOARE

Preparing the ground

Let me sing for my beloved my love-song concerning his vineyard: My beloved had a vineyard on a very fertile hill. He dug it and cleared it of stones, and planted it with choice vines; he built a watch-tower in the midst of it, and hewed out a wine vat in it; he expected it to yield grapes, but it yielded wild grapes.

St Cuthbert was a seventh-century bishop of Lindisfarne, an island off the coast of Northumbria. Although an Anglo-Saxon, he had been educated in the Celtic tradition at the abbey of Melrose in the Scottish Borders. As a young man, Cuthbert was a shepherd and his call to give himself to God came in AD651, when he had a vision on the night that St Aidan, the great missionary to Northumbria, died.

Cuthbert became a monk, and all his life loved to simply be with God in solitude. He felt deeply the tension of being a bishop and living a public role, but the soil of his upbringing and training as a monk stood him in good stead, equipping him and enabling him to have a fruitful ministry until he died. His legacy of preaching and teaching, spiritual guidance and reconciliation was huge and lasting on the Christian church and beyond.

Lent is all about preparing the ground for future growth and fruitfulness: clearing away the rubbish, fertilising the soil, watering and planting. These are springtime garden tasks, but they apply equally to the garden of the soul. The 'beloved' in today's reading, who is God himself in Isaiah's parable, did all this in expectation of a good harvest to come. So imagine his disappointment when wild grapes were all his reward. Isaiah is demonstrating God's care for Israel and his grief at the lack of fruitful growth because the people did not listen or respond to his love.

God prepared Cuthbert as a shepherd so that he was open to God's invitation when it came. He then taught him to put down deep roots in prayer and obedience as a monk. These preparations helped him to let go of the things that would distract him from a fruitful life.

How will we use this time of Lent to tend the vineyard of our soul?

LIZ HOARE

Turning towards the light

Now my head is lifted up above my enemies all around me, and I will offer in his tent sacrifices with shouts of joy; I will sing and make melody to the Lord. Hear, O Lord, when I cry aloud, be gracious to me and answer me! 'Come,' my heart says, 'seek his face!' Your face, Lord, do I seek. Do not hide your face from me.

When I moved into my current vicarage to start a new ministry as parish priest, the diocese decided to give my driveway a makeover. Fresh tarmac was laid down, and it seemed that a good job had been done. I was sad to learn soon after, however, that the drive had hitherto been thick with daffodils along its edges every spring. While renewing the driveway, the tarmac company had also widened it, and it looked unlikely that the daffodils would ever be seen again. Imagine my delight when the following spring small shoots began to poke up through the tarmac, eventually growing tall and green and topped with beautiful yellow flowers. Propelled by the need to seek the light, the bulbs had pushed their way through the barrier to grow upwards towards the sunlight that they needed to survive.

It is an Easter image I never tire of, for it speaks of the power of the resurrection to bring life and hope where there previously was neither. In the same way Jesus burst forth from the tomb on the first Easter Day, because death could not hold him.

As plants turn towards the sun, the source of their being, so we are designed to look towards our loving creator in worship and obedience. Repentance involves acknowledgement that we have turned away, but in confessing our sins we turn back to face God's outstretched arms of forgiveness and mercy once again. One day, we will stand before our Lord with upturned faces and never have to turn away again.

Spend some time in quiet prayer today in the presence of the one who gazes on you with love, and open up your heart to receive his life and light within you.

LIZ HOARE

Courage to live again

Nicodemus said to him, 'How can anyone be born after having grown old? Can one enter a second time into the mother's womb and be born?' Jesus answered, 'Very truly, I tell you, no one can enter the kingdom of God without being born of water and Spirit... The wind blows where it chooses, and you hear the sound of it, but you do not know where it comes from or where it goes. So it is with everyone who is born of the Spirit.'

I imagine Nicodemus as a world-weary and rather cynical religious leader who had lost the sparkle he once knew when he began his studies of God's law. Not only had he lost that early exhilaration, but he had also lost the ability to imagine that anything could be different. But Jesus, with his talk of new birth, the wind of the Spirit and the image of the serpent (v. 14), so familiar to a student of the scriptures, held out the promise of fresh green shoots once more.

What did Nicodemus need to change? Did he need courage to believe that it was possible? There is something about spring that evokes courageous action, as tiny shoots poke through tired old twigs as they push towards the light. Or perhaps he simply needed a wake-up call to embrace the life on offer once more.

The images of the Holy Spirit and new birth take us back to our baptism or whenever we first committed our lives to Christ, and the promise of growth from that beginning. It is a lifelong process, whereby we learn to live in tune with God working within us and around us, inviting us to get on board with his purposes.

Jesus criticised the Pharisees for knowing how to read the weather but missing the signs of the kingdom that were all around them. Here, Jesus spoke to Nicodemus personally with the invitation to live again. The thaw begins, for winter is past and resurrection calls. It is never too late to begin again.

What prevents you from surrendering to the Spirit of God in your life today?

LIZ HOARE

Learning to read the signs

'From the fig tree learn its lesson: as soon as its branch becomes tender and puts forth its leaves, you know that summer is near. So also, when you see all these things, you know that [the Son of Man] is near, at the very gates. Truly I tell you, this generation will not pass away until all these things have taken place. Heaven and earth will pass away, but my words will not pass away.'

In some parts of the world, the seasons move quickly from summer to winter and spring and autumn are barely noticeable. In the northern hemisphere the seasons are more distinct; there is even an official start date for spring.

Nevertheless, it is difficult to say exactly when it has begun. There may be a mild sunny day when our hopes rise only to crash again as the cold returns. Spring can be unpredictable. One year it arrives early while another year it seems as though it will never come. Even so, we can learn to read the signs. There are reliable sequences, such as snowdrops being followed by crocuses and daffodils. Other signs are less predictable – will the oak blossom before the ash this year or the ash before the oak?

In Matthew 24, Jesus is speaking about events that would soon come to pass as well as events far off in the future. He warned his disciples about being misled by those making false claims to be the Messiah. Instead, the disciples were instructed to watch for signs of the kingdom and to always be ready for Jesus' unexpected return (v. 44). Just as spring puts forth its signs, reassuring us that it will come, so the signs described by Jesus are designed to help us to trust his word and to live as those who are always prepared. Learning to read the signs of the times is part of growing in Christian maturity and wisdom.

What are the signs around your life at present that reassure you that Jesus is faithful to his word? Pray for eyes to see and ears to hear.

LIZ HOARE

Growing towards maturity

But speaking the truth in love, we must grow up in every way into him who is the head, into Christ, from whom the whole body, joined and knitted together by every ligament with which it is equipped, as each part is working properly, promotes the body's growth in building itself up in love.

Like the readings from Ephesians 3 and John 15 last week (see 15 and 16 March), these verses with their body imagery have much to teach us about spiritual growth and maturity. Just as we need to put down deep roots and abide in Christ, we are also meant to grow upwards into him. We do not want to remain seeds in the ground, nor do we want to emerge only to find our growth is stunted for want of warmth, light and nutrients. God provides us with all that we need to grow – not least, as our reading suggests, others to keep us company and complement our place in Christ's body.

These metaphors of earthly growth help us to understand spiritual maturity as Paul understood it and also what it is the Holy Spirit is drawing us towards. Together, we are members of Christ and all have a part to play in the growth of his body on earth. Think of growth as becoming what we are meant to be. It is the Holy Spirit who works within us to enable growth to take place. A crocus bulb will not produce a daffodil; a runner bean will not grow into a cucumber. It comes as a relief to realise that God is not saying, 'Why aren't you like x or y?' (and here we can put someone's name whom we admire or who seems a much 'better' Christian than we are). God may well be asking, however, 'Why aren't you becoming the person I made you to be?'

We all have limitations. Shy primroses peep out from near the earth. Hollyhocks grow tall and flamboyant. The world is richer for both.

The medieval mystic, Meister Eckhart, who died c. 1328, said God has planted a seed in each one of us and we are the womb that will bring it to birth. What are the seeds that God wants to grow in you at this time?

LIZ HOARE

The Feast of the Annunciation

Elizabeth was filled with the Holy Spirit and exclaimed with a loud cry, 'Blessed are you among women, and blessed is the fruit of your womb. Any why has this happened to me, that the mother of my Lord comes to me? For as soon as I heard the sound of your greeting, the child in my womb leapt for joy. And blessed is she who believed that there would be a fulfilment of what was spoken to her by the Lord.'

In this beautiful cameo depicting the deep bond between these two women, one older and one very young, we see deep and transforming hope springing up out of difficult circumstances. Both women knew the shame of being in the public gaze, and each reached out to the other in love and support. Something new was about to take place as each woman gave birth.

Spring announces new life. Elizabeth recognised from Mary's greeting that something revolutionary was happening in her very presence. Her own baby leapt with joy in her womb, and she burst out in praise and blessing. She was alert and ready to recognise the newness and the potential of what God was doing.

We can be so preoccupied with our own concerns that we miss what God is doing in the world; new life that is emerging around us. Taking time to notice, to rejoice and to enjoy is one of the gifts that Lent holds out to us with its invitation to slow down and pay attention to what really matters.

Jesus criticised the Pharisees because they knew how to read the weather but missed the signs of the kingdom all around them. It will help us to cultivate the kind of joy and gratitude that Elizabeth expressed as we also realise that God is never absent and that there are always moments when new life is present and new possibilities may be born. Mary, for her part, was learning to grow in trust and to recognise spiritual insights of her own. Each woman used the waiting time to cultivate their hearts to receive from the Lord what he had to give them.

Dear Lord, open my spiritual eyes and ears today. Amen

LIZ HOARE

Passiontide: Mark 11—16

As well as being an excellent teacher, Jesus is also a master of the understatement. I found this to be even more true when I reread Mark's account of the Passiontide events in preparation for this series.

As I read, I discovered that Jesus had packed into those few days no fewer than six of the nine spiritual gifts which Paul lists in his writing on the subject (1 Corinthians 12). He does this not by speaking about them, but by putting them into action, as if to say to his disciples, 'This is how it should be done. These are the supernatural ways in which I will equip you to carry on where I am leaving off.'

So, for Passiontide this year, we are going to concentrate on Jesus' actions during those 14 days. What is he doing here that he wants his followers to be doing when he will no longer be with them in person? And consequently, what does he want us to be doing that we may not be doing already? As I read, I got the feeling that Jesus was providing his followers with as many examples as he could of the ways in which he wanted them to minister his love and care for the world, which he was soon to leave.

They might not have realised it at the time, but from Pentecost onwards Jesus' disciples would, in the power of the Spirit, be enabled to do everything that Jesus himself had done. What he was doing now was providing last-minute reminders of the possibilities that were to come.

The message is for us too. As his followers today, we too are inheritors of that ministry to the world. We also are equipped with the power of the Spirit. Each of those gifts which Jesus displayed over his last few days is ours to command as believers. The promise still holds. I am always conscious of how little we, as a church, seem to appreciate and put to use the power we have been given.

Why, we might ask, did Jesus choose to do it this way? Why didn't he cast out a few demons on one of those days? He could at least have told the twelve – and every believer who was to follow – that this is what they would be doing? Well, perhaps he did!

PAUL GRAVELLE

Cloak Sunday

They brought the colt to Jesus, threw their cloaks over the animal, and Jesus got on. Many people spread their cloaks on the road, while others cut branches in the field and spread them on the road. The people who were in front and those who followed behind began to shout, 'Praise God! God bless him who comes in the name of the Lord! God bless the coming kingdom of King David, our father. Praise be to God!'

In a week's time, we shall be celebrating Palm Sunday and some of us will be taking part in processions with palm branches and many will be receiving palm crosses. I often wonder why, because the story is all about cloaks and not much about palms. For Middle Eastern peasants in those days, their cloaks would have been a most valuable asset. Quite apart from its value as a universal garment in all kinds of weather, it would serve as bedding at night and as a temporary shelter when travelling.

There were two kinds of people in the crowd which gathered to acclaim Jesus as Messiah. Some were there for a cheap thrill, so it seemed. They wanted to make a gesture like everyone else, so they, somewhat thoughtlessly I feel, tore branches off the trees to make a cheap, disposable pathway for the royal donkey.

But what had others done? They had spread their cloaks – yes, their precious cloaks – on the dusty road! Jesus' disciples had contributed cloaks to adorn the humble donkey, but these folk – and many of them would have been peasants coming into Jerusalem for the Passover – had sacrificed far more than that. What would their cloaks be like after everyone had gone by!

I know I am sometimes to be found taking the cheapest, easiest, fastest way to achieve something that really needs much more from me. It is never easy to make the kind of sacrifice we ought, whether it is in cash, time or labour, when a cheaper way offers itself. What would you have done if you had been there?

Lord, help me not to hold on to my cloak too tightly,
and not to damage anyone's trees either. Amen

PAUL GRAVELLE

Anything you ask?

Jesus answered them, 'Have faith in God. I assure you that whoever tells this hill to get up and throw itself in the sea and does not doubt in his heart, but believes that what he says will happen, it will be done for him. For this reason I tell you: When you pray and ask for something, believe that you have received it, and you will be given whatever you ask for.'

This is one of the 'difficult sayings' of Jesus. I remember trying to read a book on this subject and having to set it down unfinished because I couldn't cope with what it said. It is only now, many years later, that I realise Jesus is speaking about two of the spiritual gifts which Paul lists in his first letter to the young church in Corinth: the gifts of faith and miracles (1 Corinthians 12:9–10). I have learnt now that these two gifts always work together. First, Jesus says here, 'Have faith in God.' In other words, wait for God to give you the absolute conviction that he is about to act. This is the spiritual gift of faith which Paul talks about. When you are given that gift, then act – because a miracle is more than likely to happen if you do!

Peter had this gift when he healed the lame man at the temple gate in Acts 3, and we are being taught here to expect God to continue to act in that way. Miracles are a cooperative act between God and attentive followers. I often complain that we see so few miracles today, but how often have followers like you and I been given the gift of faith – but failed to respond to it?

When Jesus speaks about moving mountains, we think about *mountain-moving* faith as being something way beyond our capability. But when the conviction is there – the conviction that God is ready to act – the moment has come to speak the miracle into being, and to say, like Peter, 'In the name of Jesus Christ of Nazareth...' (Acts 3:6)

Lord, make me ready to recognise the gift of faith
and give me the courage to act when it comes.

PAUL GRAVELLE

A gift of wisdom

Some Pharisees and some members of Herod's party were sent to Jesus to trap him with questions. They came to him and said... 'Tell us, is it against our Law to pay taxes to the Roman Emperor? Should we pay them or not?' But Jesus saw through their trick and answered... 'Bring a silver coin, and let me see it?' They brought him one, and he asked, 'Whose face and name are these?' 'The Emperor's,' they answered. So Jesus said, 'Well, then, pay to the Emperor what belongs to the Emperor, and pay to God what belongs to God.' And they were amazed at Jesus.

Yesterday we encountered Jesus speaking about the gifts of faith and miracles. In today's passage, we find him using another of the gifts of the Spirit – the gift of wisdom. This gift is usually given when we encounter opposition and find ourselves in a tight spot. The opposition certainly thought they had Jesus neatly cornered with their question about paying tax. But what a wise and beautiful answer Jesus gave them! This incident is a perfect example of the gift of wisdom.

Jesus promises his followers, 'I will give you such words and wisdom that none of your enemies will be able to refute or contradict what you say' (Luke 21:15). This was certainly true for Stephen, the first Christian martyr, of whom it is said, 'the Spirit gave [him] such wisdom that when he spoke, they could not refute him' (Acts 6:10). It sounds as if the gift was definitely with Stephen, but I have also heard of this gift being evident in places, such as parts of Africa and India today, where the persecution of Christians is commonplace.

I wonder if you have ever experienced this gift yourself? There are many situations in which Christians find themselves where a word which silences those in opposition would be more than appropriate. If you are faced with those who are actively opposed to the faith in Jesus Christ for which you stand, this is the gift you should ask for.

'This power working in us is the same as the mighty strength which he used when he raised Christ from death' (Ephesians 1:19).

PAUL GRAVELLE

Giving everything

As Jesus sat near the Temple treasury, he watched the people as they dropped in their money. Many rich men dropped in a lot of money; then a poor widow came along and dropped in two little copper coins, worth about a penny. He called his disciples together and said to them, 'I tell you that this poor widow put more in the offering box than all the others. For the others put in what they had to spare of their riches; but she, poor as she is, put in all she had – she gave all she had to live on.'

Here is another example of Jesus demonstrating one of the nine spiritual gifts. This time it is the gift of knowledge that he uses to teach his disciples a lesson about giving. While the difference between the widow and the earlier givers to the treasury would have been apparent from their appearance, only by a special revelation could Jesus have known that those two tiny coins represented everything that she had left.

This gift is invaluable in counselling situations, or whenever we find ourselves called to pray for someone but don't know how. Whatever else he may have done to help the poor widow, Jesus used the special knowledge he was given about her desperate situation to teach a lesson about commitment to the disciples in the first place – and also to us, his 21st-century followers. He didn't need to add another word. The previous givers could easily have afforded their donations to the temple treasury. The widow was suddenly and entirely dependent on God to provide for her. Her commitment to God was total. Jesus lets that lesson sink in without further comment.

We may feel uncomfortable to be left like that. What does he expect of us? Are we called to sell everything and give to the poor? A wealthy man was once told to do exactly that by Jesus, wasn't he?

What does this story mean for you? Perhaps it is not about money at all, but about another kind of commitment, more about the degree of dependence that we place on our God or about having every aspect of our lives committed to Jesus?

PAUL GRAVELLE

Some end-time words

And when you are arrested and taken to court, do not worry ahead of time about what you are going to say; when the time comes, say whatever is then given to you. For the words you speak will not be yours; they will come from the Holy Spirit. Men will hand over their own brothers to be put to death, and fathers will do the same to their children. Children will turn against their parents and have them put to death.

The whole of Mark 13 is given over to Jesus speaking about the time of his coming again, ending with the warning that 'no one knows… when that day or hour will come'.

The interesting thing here is that Jesus gives us a clear definition of the spiritual gift of wisdom, which we found him using himself in the passage from Mark 12 two days ago. Who knows when it may come about that we find ourselves faced with this kind of situation. There are places in today's world where people are arrested for possession of Christian literature. The spiritual gift of wisdom could well be manifested in many instances that never come to our ears!

Sadly, Jesus' prophecy about family betrayals is coming to pass far too often today. I have read about a girl in Uzbekistan who was thrown out of her home by her parents because she had become a Christian evangelist. This is by no means unusual. As well as the persecuted and the imprisoned, Christians disowned by their families are very much a reality today and are much deserving and needful of our prayers.

We have been thinking about spiritual gifts. Let's not overlook the gift of prayer language, or 'tongues', as the Bible calls it. Using this, we can pray effectively for people like these, whose precise needs and circumstances we do not know. It is for such purposes as this that God gives us this gift, through the power of his Spirit, and we need to use it for the sake of these, our persecuted brothers and sisters, if for no other reason.

Praying 'in the Spirit' is said by Paul to 'edify'
or build up growing Christians.

PAUL GRAVELLE

The jar of perfume

Jesus was in Bethany at the house of Simon, a man who had suffered from a dreaded skin disease. While Jesus was eating, a woman came in with an alabaster jar full of a very expensive perfume... She broke the jar and poured the perfume on Jesus' head. Some of the people there became angry and said to one another, 'What was the use of wasting the perfume? It could have been sold... and the money given to the poor!'

Simon, the host at this gathering, would likely have been someone whom Jesus had healed. We could say that he is an example of the spiritual gift of healing being used by Jesus. We will, however, find another example of this the day after tomorrow. Today's story finds the other guests – and Matthew tells us that the disciples were all there – criticising the lavishing of expensive perfume on Jesus. It seems they have learned nothing from their experience in the temple with the poor widow. Nothing is too good when it comes to giving to God, be it the only two coins one has left or a treasured jar of perfume.

But there is something in this story which speaks to me about worship. The perfume was a personal gift for Jesus alone, an offering from that woman's heart, a pure act of worship. Do we tend to think of worship as singing songs in church? I sometimes find myself singing those songs without recognising whether they are directed personally *to* God or are just *about* him. Personally, if I want to worship my God, I need to address him directly!

In the story, Jesus recognises that this is exactly what is happening. The woman's act is one of pure worship, and I try to follow her example in church when we have a song that speaks directly to God. I will even do this to the extent that I stop singing if there are words that are beyond what I feel able to say at that moment.

Try it for yourself when you are next in church.
I hope you won't have to leave too many lines out!

PAUL GRAVELLE

Gifts of prophecy

Then Jesus sent two of [his disciples] with these instructions: 'Go into the city, and a man carrying a jar of water will meet you. Follow him to the house he enters, and say to the owner of the house, "The Teacher says, Where is the room where my disciples and I will eat the Passover meal?" Then he will show you a large upstairs room, fixed up and furnished, where you will get everything ready for us.' The disciples left, went to the city, and found everything just as Jesus had told them; and they prepared the Passover meal.

It is true that biblical prophecy is 'more forthtelling than foretelling'. But here is an instance where Jesus uses the gift of prophecy in the latter way. And more foretelling is to come, because it is at the Passover meal that Jesus will tell Peter that he will deny him three times.

However, it is the forthtelling aspect of prophecy which Jesus also displays at the meal, which has had the most lasting effect upon us, because his prophetic words have been echoed at every celebration of Holy Communion, down the ages and across the globe: 'This bread… is my body; this cup… is my blood.'

The spiritual gift of prophecy occurs whenever God speaks through human lips. Many of us may have felt that this has happened when we feel that we have said just the right thing in a particular situation. There are, however, those times when you feel an urge to speak, whether to a few or to many, and you know that urge comes from God.

Paul tells us that prophetic words of a forthtelling nature will always bring help, encouragement or comfort (1 Corinthians 14:3), so this is a useful test for us to use before and even as we speak. But, to my shame, there are far too many times when the words I have been given have remained unspoken. Do you ever feel the same, I wonder? Two verses later, Paul implies that this is the most important of all the gifts of the Spirit, so it is something to which we should give serious attention; perhaps by using Samuel's prayer:

'Speak, Lord, your servant is listening' (1 Samuel 3:9).

PAUL GRAVELLE

Betrayal

As soon as Judas arrived, he went up to Jesus and said, 'Teacher!' and kissed him. So they arrested Jesus and held him tight. But one of those standing there drew his sword and struck at the High Priest's slave, cutting off his ear… Then all the disciples left [Jesus] and ran away. A certain young man, wearing only a linen cloth, was following Jesus. They tried to arrest him, but he ran away naked, leaving the cloth behind.

I need to slip in a verse from Luke's account, because Luke, being a doctor, doesn't overlook that Jesus performed a miracle of healing right in this moment. Luke writes that Jesus 'touched the man's ear and healed him' (Luke 22:51). So we add healing to our list of spiritual gifts used by Jesus in his final days. It happened instantly, and it is sometimes said that if healing is instant, it is a miracle. However, healing may also take time, as with the blind man who, at first, only saw people 'like trees walking' (Mark 8:24). In any case, we cannot leave such a verse unchallenged in the light of Jesus' teaching. Violence is not the answer to any situation.

The question many ask is: 'Was Judas' betrayal really necessary?' There certainly seem to have been enough people who wanted to see Jesus crucified without involving one of his own disciples. Theologians have discussed and reflected upon this for a long time, yet we should be careful not to allow ourselves to fall into such a state of dissatisfaction that we become enemies of the Saviour himself. It is also very easy to betray him when we are in a crowd of unbelievers!

The verses about the young man who fled the scene naked add such a beautifully human touch. The young man might even have been Mark himself!

I recently read a report by a group of historians which added eight fresh proofs of the authenticity of the gospel narratives. One of the words they use to describe the authenticity of the narratives reported in the gospels was 'unimpeachable'. I can't think of a better one.

Lord, keep me from situations where I might even be tempted to betray you.

PAUL GRAVELLE

The kangaroo court

Then Jesus was taken to the High Priest's house, where all the chief priests, the elders, and the teachers of the Law were gathering… Many witnesses told lies against Jesus, but their stories did not agree… The High Priest stood up in front of them all and questioned Jesus… But Jesus kept quiet and would not say a word. Again, the High Priest questioned him, 'Are you the Messiah, the Son of the Blessed God?' 'I am,' answered Jesus.

This was a kangaroo court if ever there was one! There was not a quorum of the council, and they could not find two witnesses whose testimony agreed, as required in Jewish law. Besides that, this midnight assembly did not have the power of the death penalty, which they subsequently imposed for the crime of blasphemy – which, even under Jewish law, Jesus had not in fact committed.

Did you ever behave like the members of this hastily assembled pseudo-court before you believed? Did you ever criticise the claims of Jesus without examining what they really were? I know I did, and I can understand where people are coming from when they say that they 'don't do church,' are 'not into the Jesus thing' or something similar. It is simply a case of taking an honest look at who Jesus was and what his claims are. As C.S. Lewis put it, he is either mad, or the devil from hell, or he is exactly who he claims to be. The correct answer to the question of Jesus' identity is the gateway to eternal life. I often think of Thomas as the first true Christian when he fell on his knees, as I'm sure he must have done, and addressed the newly risen Lord Jesus as 'My Lord and my God.'

There are places in this world today where behaving overtly as a Christian can incur a verdict of 'blasphemy', exactly after the pattern of Jesus. The difference is that these are genuine civil or police courts and will more likely involve a fine or imprisonment than a death sentence.

Pray for Christians who live under persecution, that the Lord who suffered similar injustice will bring them release and freedom.

PAUL GRAVELLE

Been there!

Peter was still down in the courtyard when one of the High Priest's servant women came by. When she saw Peter warming himself, she looked straight at him and said, 'You too, were with Jesus of Nazareth.' But he denied it. 'I don't know... I don't understand what you are talking about,' he answered, and went out into the passageway. Just then a rooster crowed.

Annie Vallotton's line drawing of this incident, which enriches the Good News Bible, shows Peter sitting before the fire with his hands raised in surrender to the servant woman's pointing finger. It gives the impression that he is taking the easy way out of the situation. Taking the easy option can so easily be the route we take in some situations. Church this Sunday? It's a wet day; I think I'll give it a miss this time. A beggar outside the supermarket? Walk straight on; she'll only spend any money I give her on drugs.

There was nothing supernatural about the rooster's crowing; dawn would have been about to break by then. But Peter, we discover, wept bitterly for his failing and subsequently went on to work signs and miracles in the name of Jesus, bringing thousands of believers into the church. He surrendered, not to the easy way out, but to the call of the Holy Spirit, carrying on the work that Jesus had demonstrated.

I have certainly been where Peter was in that courtyard, and I suspect that we all have, if we have had any experience of life as believers. Failure is all too easy. But, as Peter discovered, reconciliation is always waiting. God's supply of forgiveness is boundless, and the opportunity to follow in Peter's footsteps lies at our doorstep. We have been reading about some of the spiritual gifts which Jesus used during the last days of his ministry. These are available for us to use through the power of the Holy Spirit.

Reconciliation between Peter and the risen Jesus resulted in Peter being told to feed Jesus' sheep. This remains our calling too. We cannot fulfil it in the way Jesus intends without using those spiritual gifts he offers us.

Jesus' words were confirmed by the signs he performed.
His successors followed this same pattern.

PAUL GRAVELLE

Barabbas and I

At every Passover Festival Pilate was in the habit of setting free any one prisoner the people asked for. At that time a man named Barabbas was in prison with the rebels who had committed murder in the riot. When the crowd gathered and began to ask Pilate for the usual favour, he asked them, 'Do you want me to set free for you the king of the Jews?'... But the chief priests stirred up the crowd to ask, instead, that Pilate set Barabbas free for them. Pilate spoke again to the crowd, 'What, then, do you want me to do with the one you call the king of the Jews?' They shouted back, 'Crucify him!'... Pilate wanted to please the crowd, so he set Barabbas free for them. Then he had Jesus whipped and handed him over to be crucified.

Barabbas knew what to expect: first the whipping. The whip was called a scourge – it had several lashes, like the infamous 'cat o' nine tails'. Each 'tail' featured sharp metal pieces embedded at intervals, designed to tear the skin off your back long before the flogging was over. Then those Roman lower ranks could do what they liked with you. Barabbas reckoned he would have to carry the crossbar over his raw shoulders all the way to the place of execution and then wait while they assembled the cross. The soldiers would bind him tightly and nail him down. Barabbas could hardly bear to think beyond that point, but he knew that the worst was still to come.

But, amazingly, none of that happened. The jailors came along and let him off, scot-free! And it was an innocent person, Jesus, the Son of God himself, who had to go through it all instead. We know, of course, that it was not just instead of Barabbas, but instead of each one of us that Jesus went to the cross.

Each of us stands in Barabbas' shoes. When we sing songs which recall or simply say that Jesus 'was crucified for us under Pontius Pilate', we should experience a frisson of terror at what the alternative might have held for us. And then, we can thank God for sending Jesus in our place.

Thank you, Lord God, that, as believers in Jesus the Christ,
we can look forward with complete confidence to resurrection
and the life of the world to come!

PAUL GRAVELLE

109

Nine o'clock in the morning

Then they crucified him and divided his clothes among themselves, throwing dice to see who would get which piece of clothing. It was nine o'clock in the morning when they crucified him. The notice of the accusation against him said: 'The King of the Jews.' They also crucified two bandits with Jesus, one on his right and the other on his left. People passing by shook their heads and hurled insults at Jesus... And the two who were crucified with Jesus insulted him also.

There was to be another, far happier, 'nine o'clock in the morning' before long, of course – on the Day of Pentecost. But for now, let's look at what was happening on that hot, dusty hill, not far from Herod's palace. The Roman crucifixion squad had carried out their main task. The victims had been stripped naked, bound and nailed firmly to their crosses. Then came the tough job of hoisting those heavy crosses upright and thumping them down into the holes they had already dug. Now it was time to slip off their close-fitting helmets and sit down for a bit of relaxation – gambling for the prisoners' clothes.

Had they taken in what Pilate had ordered to be written above Jesus' head? Being ordinary legionaries, could they even read? The passers-by and the crucified bandits seemed to get the point. 'Some king!' was what they were thinking as they hurled their jibes. This was the culmination of the burden that Jesus chose to endure. Along with the terrible beating he had gone through, the crippling journey along the *Via Dolorosa*, the shame of being stripped naked in public view and the unbelievable pain of being physically nailed to and literally hung up to die on a wooden cross, now came the rude insults from people, some of whom may even have shouted, 'Hosanna' in his honour only a few days before.

There is story told of an unbeliever who was once challenged to stand in front of a life-size crucifix and say three times, 'You did all that for me, and I couldn't care less!' Needless to say, it is said that he failed the test.

Crucified Saviour, naked God, you hang disgraced and powerless.
Grieving, we dare to hope as we wait at the cross.

PAUL GRAVELLE

Reality!

At noon the whole country was covered with darkness, which lasted for three hours… With a loud cry Jesus died. The curtain hanging in the emple was torn in two, from top to bottom. The army officer who was standing there in front of the cross saw how Jesus had died. 'This man was really the Son of God!' he said.

Mark records two supernatural events which accompanied Jesus' death: the hours of darkness in the middle of the day, and the amazing splitting of the curtain which shielded the sacred 'holy of holies' in the temple. It 'was torn in two, from top to bottom', as if by the hands of God. This was to signify that, through the death of Jesus, everyone now has direct access to God the Father. The curtain which previously kept God at a distance had been torn open. Have a look at what the other gospel-writers say about the happenings of that day. Each one adds something of intense interest to Mark's account which give us cause to pause and wonder.

The Roman officer in the story instantly saw through that curtain! The very way in which Jesus died showed him the truth. He was convinced that this man, hanging crucified in front of him, was no less than the Son of God himself. He might not have realised it yet, but he was one of those who had qualified for eternal life through simply believing. I wonder how he progressed with his newly discovered belief.

There are always those who are struck by the awe of an occasion like Good Friday and even make decisions to change their lives because of what Christ has done for them. Then, a few weeks, or even days, down the track, they have slipped back to their previous way of life. Let's pray for those who, like the Roman army officer, recognise Jesus as the Son of God on this day – that they will hold to the faith which they grasp today and never let it go.

Lord God, you know each one who will respond to the story of the death of your Son this Good Friday. Hold them fast by the power of your Spirit and bring them safely through to eternal life. Amen

PAUL GRAVELLE

Instructions for believers

Last of all, Jesus appeared to the eleven disciples as they were eating…
He said to them, 'Go throughout the whole world and preach the gospel
to all people. Whoever believes and is baptised will be saved… Believers
will be given the power to perform miracles: they will drive out demons
in my name; they will speak in strange tongues; if they pick up snakes or
drink any poison, they will not be harmed; they will place their hands on
sick people, and these will get well.'

I know it is not quite Easter yet, but we're going to take a peep into the
future, which Mark gives us at the end of his gospel. This is part of the longer
of the two endings which are given to us in modern translations. Although
the command that the risen Lord Jesus gives about preaching the gospel to
all people appears to have been given primarily to the disciples, there is no
doubt at all that the instructions which follow are specifically to believers.
And that, of course, includes you and me!

No matter how hard we try, we cannot escape the fact that, if we claim to
believe, these are the things we should be doing. I challenge myself about
this continuously and look for opportunities to exercise the power which
is latent in every baptised Christian.

To my knowledge, I have never heard this passage read in church. Is
the church at large afraid of the supernatural? Have we all become a little
fearful about bringing Jesus' instructions into the present?

But we are about to celebrate the resurrection of Jesus: the most amazingly supernatural event of all time. We say, in all our Christian creeds, that
we believe this to be true. The promises that the risen Jesus makes to us
as believers in this passage are true as well. They stand today, as they have
stood for all saints and believers ever since.

---

*Lord Jesus Christ, in your resurrection power equip your church with the
gifts of your Holy Spirit, so that the world may hear and know that you are
God of God and Lord of Lords in the glory of the Father. Amen*

PAUL GRAVELLE

Easter

Christians believe that one day we will meet Jesus face to face. He will be in his resurrected body, and we will be in ours. The Easter story brings us closer to this truth: each appearance of Jesus to his friends and followers offers a tiny hint of what that meeting could be like.

We see how Jesus' body is both different yet the same. He appears behind locked doors, but cooks and eats. He is sometimes unrecognisable, yet he is solid and scarred and unmistakably himself. We see his loving greetings to his friends: his way of striking straight to the heart of their doubts and painful memories to bring peace, joy and relief. Not only can his risen body come to them wherever their grief and fear has taken them, but his words can find out the secrets of their hearts. Jesus connects very personally with his followers, comforting, convincing and calling them in ways that are selected by the one who knows them best.

Often there is something in these encounters that echoes a previous moment from that person's experience of Jesus, whether it is spectacular, like the miraculous catch of fish, or simple, like the breaking of bread. The resurrected Jesus uses these recollections to recall his disciples and to renew their relationship with him. There is comfort for past grief, and forgiveness for past hurts. After their meeting with the risen Jesus, each follower has a new sense of their purpose in this new kingdom. Often, they have a specific task to do.

As we read the stories again, I invite you to catch a glimpse of the Jesus who will one day greet you in the same way. Imagine what that moment could be like. He knows you and loves you completely, and he died to make this meeting possible.

This Easter may the risen Jesus find you wherever you are. May his words speak straight to your unspoken needs and hopes. May his peace transform you and give you fresh purpose, and may you know the joy of following him wherever he wants you to go.

AMY SCOTT ROBINSON

Rising before the sun

Early on the first day of the week, while it was still dark, Mary Magdalene came to the tomb and saw that the stone had been removed from the tomb. So she ran and went to Simon Peter and the other disciple… and said to them, 'They have taken the Lord out of the tomb, and we do not know where they have laid him.' Then Peter and the other disciple set out and went towards the tomb… Then the other disciple… also went in, and he saw and believed; for as yet they did not understand the scripture, that he must rise from the dead. Then the disciples returned to their homes.

How many times must I have read this passage in my lifetime? Yet I have always skimmed past the five words that set the scene: 'While it was still dark.' Contrasting with our celebration of a bright Easter morning – all those cards covered in daffodils and sunshine – the story of Jesus' resurrection begins in the dark. His friends are grieving, sleep-deprived and confused. Mary Magdalene assumes that somebody has removed Jesus' body from the tomb and hidden it. Meanwhile, although Peter and John 'believe' on seeing the folded graveclothes, they do not understand. Their belief at this point is no more than a willingness to accept a mystery. After their frantic race to the tomb comes a moment of anticlimax when they both return home. With all they had witnessed of Jesus, perhaps there was a spark of hope in them on hearing Mary's news, but at this point it seems quickly snuffed out. I imagine the pair of them trudging away again, telling Mary that they are going to get some more sleep; they will see what they can find out when the sun comes up.

We can be so worn down by bad news that the most difficult thing to believe is good news. It is hard to hope when it is still dark. We, like Peter and John, can become disoriented by relentless darkness in the news and in our lives, until we struggle to remember what we have been told to look for and we begin to draw the worst possible conclusions from every situation. But with Jesus, even while it is still dark, it is safe to assume the best.

The greatest moment in history took place in the dark. He is risen indeed – alleluia!

In the darkness, may we remember and reach for you, our light.

AMY SCOTT ROBINSON

Called by name

But Mary stood weeping outside the tomb. As she wept, she bent over to look into the tomb; and she saw two angels in white, sitting where the body of Jesus had been lying… She turned round and saw Jesus standing there, but she did not know that it was Jesus… Supposing him to be the gardener, she said to him, 'Sir, if you have carried him away, tell me where you have laid him, and I will take him away.' Jesus said to her, 'Mary!' She turned and said to him in Hebrew, 'Rabbouni!' (which means Teacher).

If you could hear your name called right now, by anybody at all, whose voice would it be? And what tone of voice would you want to hear? Our names can sound comforting when spoken softly by a friend, full of magic when murmured by a lover, exciting when called across a crowd by an unexpected but familiar voice.

The angels had not been there before. A few moments earlier, Peter and John had been standing in the tomb, looking at the folded graveclothes. There had not been anything else to see. But now they had both gone, and Mary bent down for another despairing look at the place that she knew would be empty; but it was not. After her brief conversation with the two figures – at what point did she realise they were angels? – she turned and saw, through her tears and the early dawn shadows, a third figure. She assumed he was the gardener, until he said her name.

This private scene in the garden after the two disciples have returned home is the picture of a calling: profoundly personal and infinitely loving, the risen Jesus choosing Mary to be the first bearer of the good news of his resurrection. It is also a picture of two friends reunited. They know each other so well. That two-word exchange of recognition must have been accompanied by a hundred unspoken messages: the look of wonder on Mary's face, the love and reassurance in Jesus' eyes.

We worship a risen Lord who knows us by name and who calls us each individually to take up our part in his plans for the world. Let us listen for his familiar voice.

Imagine Jesus calling your name.
How does he say it? How will you respond?

AMY SCOTT ROBINSON

To those who have not seen

Although the doors were shut, Jesus came and stood among them and said, 'Peace be with you.' Then he said to Thomas, 'Put your finger here and see my hands. Reach out your hand and put it in my side. Do not doubt but believe.' Thomas answered him, 'My Lord and my God!' Jesus said to him, 'Have you believed because you have seen me? Blessed are those who have not seen and yet have come to believe.'

Jesus is talking about us, you know. We have not seen; we were not there. Two thousand years later, some of us still have not witnessed any miracles or had any experience that we feel we can put down to direct divine intervention. Some of us feel we have missed out. We were not in the right room at the right time. We do not seem to share the experiences others get so excited about. But we still believe, and Jesus calls us blessed.

Why did Jesus leave Thomas out the first time? Can we assume that it was not a mistake, that in fact Jesus knew the exact moment when Thomas had popped out to the shop? Perhaps Jesus knew what Thomas needed. This faithful disciple was a straight talker who struggled with metaphor. He told Jesus he was willing to follow him to death, if only Jesus would tell him how to get there. So he was given a bit of extra time to process the news, and his own particular moment to touch and understand. And perhaps Jesus also knew that through Thomas' need to make sure, he would have a chance to speak through the centuries, to bless you and me, who have not seen and yet have come to believe.

If, like Thomas, you feel that you were out of the room when easy faith was handed out and you long to touch and see for yourself, hear Jesus' words as an offer to you. He knows just what each of us needs, too. We can ask him for it. And when we believe, we are blessed.

Lord, we are filled with longing at the thought of being able to see you, touch you, have such certainty in the reality of you. Please come into our lives in undeniable ways. Amen

AMY SCOTT ROBINSON

Déjà vu

Just after daybreak, Jesus stood on the beach; but the disciples did not know that it was Jesus. Jesus said to them, 'Children, you have no fish, have you?' They answered him, 'No.' He said to them, 'Cast the net to the right side of the boat, and you will find some.' So they cast it, and now they were not able to haul it in because there were so many fish. That disciple whom Jesus loved said to Peter, 'It is the Lord!'

Can you remember your very first meeting with your oldest friend or your partner? Do you recall where you were, what was said or how quickly you knew that this was a relationship that would last?

Peter, James and John must have remembered one of their first meetings with Jesus. He repurposed Peter's boat as a pulpit, led the fishermen to the catch of their lives and then called them to follow him and fish for people instead (Luke 5:1–10). Now, at the other end of the story, Jesus is not on the boat with them, and the disciples feel uncertain about what to do next. They have gone back to fishing for fish, and it is not going well. But with a repeat of the miracle that first called them, realisation dawns: the stranger on the shore is Jesus himself!

This affirmation of their original calling shows the disciples that things will never go back to the way they were before they met Jesus. Although Jesus may not be physically with them on the boat, he is still able to perform the same wonders and is still calling them to the same role. This appearance both reunites the fishermen with Jesus and prepares them for their future after his ascension.

Can you remember your very first meeting with Jesus or a first moment of purposely following him? Often our early enthusiasm gets lost in the daily routine or after setbacks and disappointments. Such are the peaks and valleys of the Christian life. But as you think back to those moments, know that Jesus, who is the same yesterday, today and forever, still calls you and cares for you, just as he has always done.

Jesus, come and meet us again, just as you did then. We'll look out for you.

AMY SCOTT ROBINSON

A taste of home

When they had gone ashore, they saw a charcoal fire there, with fish on it, and bread. Jesus said to them, 'Bring some of the fish that you have just caught... Come and have breakfast.' Now none of the disciples dared to ask him, "Who are you?" because they knew it was the Lord. Jesus came and took the bread and gave it to them, and did the same with the fish.

Fish pie tastes of welcome to me. My aunt Jane used to make it as the first meal of any holiday at her house. I associate it with her excitement on seeing us and with the comfort of her home after a long journey. Do not tell anyone, but I've always suspected that aunt Jane's fish pie might be my first meal in heaven.

Here are the disciples, dragging their boat and their miraculous catch of fish to the shore, ravenous after working all night. Jesus has cooked breakfast for them and the smell of it is mouth-watering. It is a meal they have shared before, probably many times, but as Jesus took the bread and fish and handed them around, how many of them remembered the day he fed 5,000 in the same way? Or, as he broke the bread, did they recall the more recent occasion of the last supper? For the disciples, this meal is recognition. They do not need anything more to persuade them that their friend Jesus really has risen again and is with them.

We are built to experience our world with every sense, and our faith works the same way. For us, Communion gives a tiny taste of a shared heavenly feast. It is a symbol of salvation, and the remembrance of a solemn and significant meal. But after the last supper came the first breakfast. Next time you settle down with your favourite homely comfort food, close your eyes for a moment and think of Jesus on the beach, cooking bread and fish. Enjoy a foretaste of the warmth and welcome that awaits.

What other foods hold memories for you?
How could you use them in prayer?

AMY SCOTT ROBINSON

What's in a name?

[Jesus said to Peter] the third time, 'Simon son of John, do you love me?' Peter felt hurt because he said to him the third time, 'Do you love me?' And he said to him, 'Lord, you know everything; you know that I love you.' Jesus said to him, 'Feed my sheep'... After this he said to him, 'Follow me.'

When we met at school, my husband's name was Gummi. I had shared a desk with him in maths for over a year before I learned his real name. He has not used that nickname for a very long time now, but occasionally an old friend will pop up and call him Gummi, and it always sounds very strange.

Jesus gave Simon a new name: Peter, meaning rock, on which Jesus would build his church. It was part of Peter's identity from his first calling. One of the most relatable characters in the gospels, Peter is impetuous, angry, questioning and often totally wrong, but always rock-like: solid and dependable. Until, that is, his threefold denial that he ever knew Jesus.

It must have been on Peter's mind as the two of them sat on the beach. It was the first time Peter had spoken to Jesus since that moment outside the high priest's house. Fed by fear of his own arrest, he had done what he had sworn he would never do. And now Jesus is calling him by his old name: Simon, son of John.

Why? Is it all over? Is he supposed to go back to being Simon the fisherman instead of the rock for Jesus' church? Has his failure cost him everything? No wonder Peter is upset.

But Jesus gives Peter three chances to declare his love, one for each of the three denials, and after each one instructs him again to feed his sheep, his church. His use of the old name is not to take away the new one, but to offer a way for Peter to choose it again for himself. By going back to the way things began, Peter can receive forgiveness and recommit himself to following Jesus.

Lord, I am sorry for the ways I have failed you. Please forgive me and let me show you once again how much I love you. I really do still want to follow you.

AMY SCOTT ROBINSON

What about...?

Peter turned and saw the disciple whom Jesus loved following them; he was the one who had reclined next to Jesus at the supper and had said, 'Lord, who is it that is going to betray you?' When Peter saw him, he said to Jesus, 'Lord, what about him?' Jesus said to him, 'If it is my will that he remain until I come, what is that to you? Follow me!'

From their race to the empty tomb onwards, there is an almost cartoonish rivalry going on between John ('the disciple whom Jesus loved') and Peter. They always follow the same pattern: John stops, takes stock and eventually understands, while Peter rushes headlong in. So John skids to a halt at the mouth of the tomb. He is the one, on the boat, who first recognises Jesus and points the other disciples towards him. Meanwhile, Peter runs into the tomb and dives into the water. And now Peter has just received an unsettling view of his own future from Jesus, and he turns around and sees John. Perhaps he wants to know whether John will share his path to martyrdom.

Peter and John were very different people, and Jesus loved them both so much. His reply to Peter makes it clear that the life of every disciple is different. Yet the paths laid out for them are not determined by the disciples, but by Jesus: 'If it is my will.'

In fact, Peter and John did go to very different deaths, as Jesus predicted. They were true to character until the end: tradition says that Peter asked to be crucified upside down as he was unworthy to share the same death as his Lord, while John went on quietly witnessing, thinking and writing into old age. They each did what was asked of them, following the way chosen for them by the one who knew and loved them best.

There are as many different ways of following Jesus as there are Christians. It can be tempting to compare our own efforts with the ones who look braver, more prayerful, more knowledgeable. In those moments, we can remember Jesus' reply to Peter. He doesn't want us to worry about someone else. All he asks is that we follow him.

Lord, you know the way. Keep my eyes on you.

AMY SCOTT ROBINSON

Paul's journey to Rome: Acts 25—29

Paul (or Saul as he was first named) is introduced to the reader of Acts as a bystander to the killing of Stephen, the first Christian martyr (Acts 7:58). Even if he took no active part in the stoning itself, Luke makes clear that he approved of it. His later attempts to suppress the new Christian movement underline this rage towards what he then saw as a threat to his religion and nation. His turnaround on the road to Damascus following his encounter with Jesus is all the more dramatic for that hate-filled beginning.

This encounter is not a moment of conversion from one faith to another. Paul's Jewish faith in the God of his ancestors remains but is changed radically by recognising Jesus as crucified Saviour and living Lord. He is given a new life-giving commission. Through the encouragement of Ananias and the gift of the Holy Spirit, he discovers his calling to bring the name of Jesus to Jews and Gentiles alike.

Thereafter the story of Acts moves outwards and the focus shifts from Peter, James and the Jerusalem church on to Paul and his companion missionaries, so much so that after chapter 15 almost all of the story revolves around Paul's missionary work. The impact of his witness in town after town is immense, forming new church communities in place after place. Chapter 20 sees Paul making his farewell to the elders of the Ephesian church, as he sets off to Jerusalem to deliver the collection the Gentile churches have raised to help the people of Judea in the grip of a famine. Paul warns them that they will not see him again.

In the closing chapters of Acts, we find Paul under arrest in Jerusalem and then brought to Felix at Caesarea before being sent to Rome. We may think that this is a sad ending to an illustrious missionary career, but Paul and God have other ideas. Luke wants to assure us that even amid the danger and distress of Paul's situation, God is still at work and the love of Christ can still be shared. As we follow Paul's story in these chapters, let's reflect on how God can do the same today in our own lives, amid the challenges, joys and heartaches of life.

TERRY HINKS

Above politics

Three days after Festus had arrived in the province, he went up from Caesarea to Jerusalem where the chief priests and the leaders of the Jews gave him a report against Paul. They appealed to him and requested, as a favour to them against Paul, to have him transferred to Jerusalem. They were, in fact, planning an ambush to kill him along the way. Festus replied that Paul was being kept at Caesarea, and that he himself intended to go there shortly.

Felix, the governor in charge of Judea, had kept Paul in prison but had engaged him in a series of conversations, fascinated with this new way of living. Then he had got cold feet and become nervous of the political consequences of becoming too involved. He drew back and left Paul languishing in prison for two years, though still allowing him to see friends.

Festus succeeded Felix as prefect and clearly wanted to make his mark and sort out the backlog of cases, including that of Paul. Festus was a careful operator and consulted with the local leaders about the case. For them, Paul remained a threat to their faith and nation, and they hatched a plot to have him transferred from Caesarea to Jerusalem and ambush him on route. Festus is obviously not taken in by the scheme. Having heard the case made by the Jerusalem leaders, he decides to go back to Caesarea to see the prisoner for himself.

In this web of political intrigue, Paul stands out as a figure of integrity and authority. Despite his dire situation his words carry courage and power. Just as Jesus confronted Pilate with his silence, Paul confronts Festus and others with carefully chosen words and a witness to a living faith that outshines all human splendour. There is a sense behind it all of human power meeting divine power.

It's been said that politics is a messy business, in which ideals clash with reality. Yet which is the greater reality here: the intrigue and plotting of the leaders or the faith of Paul? Luke knows the answer to that and shares this in the chapters to come.

---

*Learn more about your local MP or political representative
and pray for God's wisdom and integrity for them.*

TERRY HINKS

Pomp and circumstance

So on the next day Agrippa and Bernice came with great pomp, and they entered the audience hall with the military tribunes and the prominent men of the city. Then Festus gave the order and Paul was brought in. And Festus said, 'King Agrippa and all here present with us, you see this man about whom the whole Jewish community petitioned me, both in Jerusalem and here, shouting that he ought not to live any longer.'

Paul makes an appeal to the emperor, and Festus, as Caesar's representative, is obliged to send him to Rome. But first he consults King Agrippa, the local puppet king from the Herod family, who was allowed to keep the title because of his loyalty to Rome.

King Agrippa and his sister Bernice enter the hall with suitable pomp and circumstance. The focus should be on them, but instead it is on the prisoner brought before them to defend himself against the petition for his death. There is indeed an echo here of how Jesus was brought before Pilate to be questioned and judged. It is a picture that contrasts one who is in the power of others and is 'done to' with one that bears all the splendour of kingly authority and has the power of life and death. The expectation is that the one brought out is powerless and the one sitting in judgement is powerful, but the spiritual reality is different. Pilate discovered that when he met Jesus, and the same happens here. Paul waits for Agrippa's permission to speak, and when it is given, he speaks powerfully and with great freedom. The living Word is not chained, and the tables of power are turned.

However, there is a dark undercurrent to this passage, with Festus reporting the petition which seeks Paul's condemnation and execution. The noise of anger, hatred and violence hangs in the air. What must it feel like to have people believe that you should 'live no longer'? To have that weight hanging over you? Too many in our world feel that threat, because of oppressive governments, destructive ideologies, violent conflicts or abusive relationships.

Hold before God those under the threat of death today.

TERRY HINKS

Sharing hope

'All the Jews know my way of life from my youth, a life spent from the beginning among my own people and in Jerusalem. They have known for a long time, if they are willing to testify, that I have belonged to the strictest sect of our religion and lived as a Pharisee. And now I stand here on trial on account of my hope in the promise made by God to our ancestors, a promise that our twelve tribes hope to attain, as they earnestly worship day and night. It is for this hope, your Excellency, that I am accused by Jews! Why is it thought incredible by any of you that God raises the dead?'

In recent years we have become more conscious of the different cultural identities in society and their influence on our own sense of being. The popular BBC family history programme *Who Do You Think You Are?* invites celebrities to explore their family roots, to discover the stories and experiences of previous generations and so to reflect on their own identity today.

If Paul was invited on to the programme, he would be very happy to identify himself as a member of the Jewish people. He would no doubt also be appalled by the anti-Semitism of more recent centuries. His faith in Jesus did not remove his Jewish identity, but rather added to it.

Now in front of King Agrippa, he reaches out to his people, speaking of a common identity, shared religion and God-given hope. 'Hope' is the key word in this opening part of Paul's speech, and he focuses on the hope of the dead being raised by God to new life. This was a matter of debate and controversy in Judaism at the time, but the Pharisees certainly held such a hope.

Paul sees this hope confirmed in the death and resurrection of Jesus – a reality that was wholly the work of God. That promise of new life had taken on an astonishingly new and powerful deeper reality through his experience of Jesus, the Messiah, crucified Saviour and risen Lord.

Renew your hope within us, living Lord –
hope for all your children, all your creation.

TERRY HINKS

Against the name

'Indeed, I myself was convinced that I ought to do many things against the name of Jesus of Nazareth. And that is what I did in Jerusalem; with authority received from the chief priests, I not only locked up many of the saints in prison, but I also cast my vote against them when they were being condemned to death. By punishing them often in all the synagogues I tried to force them to blaspheme; and since I was so furiously enraged at them, I pursued them even to foreign cities.'

Having our deep-held beliefs challenged can be unsettling and distressing, threatening our sense of order and direction in life. At this point in his speech, Paul tells of how he saw the Jesus movement as a deadly threat to his core beliefs. There's a sense of uncontrollable anger and obsession about his pursuit of Christians from city to city, eventually taking him on to the road to Damascus. Nothing will stop him!

Anger and obsession remain part of our world today. The internet has allowed that rage to be shared far and wide. Social media sites have been found to give much more emphasis to the 'angry' emoji than the 'like' one, so feeding people's anger. Rage is such a strong emotion that it can cause loss of control and can easily be manipulated. The scenes of uprising the world saw around the US Capitol building in January 2021 are just one example of its deadly consequences.

Paul's inner rage takes him on a destructive path. He forgets what he is 'for' and focuses only on what he is 'against' – the name of Jesus and his followers. Again and again, he votes against the saints, condemning them to death. It will require an extraordinary encounter to quench this fire.

Why do we get angry? Of course, sometimes it is right to become angry; at injustice and cruelty, violence and greed. But sometimes our anger is simply an outworking of our own intolerance and prejudice, our desire to protect status and position. In time, the name that Paul had been against would take his rage away, and Paul would speak of our need to let go of anger and not allow the sun to set on it.

Where anger threatens to embitter or destroy,
bring us your healing and peace, Lord Jesus.

TERRY HINKS

Why? Who?

'With this in mind, I was travelling to Damascus with the authority and commission of the chief priests, when at midday along the road, your Excellency, I saw a light from heaven, brighter than the sun, shining around me and my companions. When we had all fallen to the ground, I heard a voice saying to me in the Hebrew language, "Saul, Saul, why are you persecuting me? It hurts you to kick against the goads." I asked, "Who are you, Lord?" The Lord answered, "I am Jesus whom you are persecuting."'

This is the breakthrough moment for Paul, the moment of encounter with the living Jesus, whom he had rejected as a false and dead Messiah. The meeting is so vital to Luke's story of Paul that it is repeated three times (first in Acts 9, then Acts 22 and finally here). The confrontation is first and foremost with the suffering Jesus – the Jesus of the cross, who identifies himself with the suffering of his followers and the suffering of humanity. Jesus even identifies with Paul's own internal suffering, telling him how he is hurting himself by his anger and denial, like a stubborn ox kicking against its owners' sharp stick.

The question 'Why' echoes down the centuries in every situation of grief and pain, of senseless violence and hatred. Why do human beings inflict such damage on each other and the natural order? Jesus continues to ask that question today, alongside so many in our world.

The deeply human question 'Why?' with all its anguish and compassion leads Paul to ask the question 'Who?' Who is this one who takes the suffering of the world on his own shoulders? Paul recognises authority in the voice and asks, 'Who are you, Lord?' This is a divine encounter, and Jesus replies with the words that John's gospel uses so powerfully – the spiritually charged words 'I am.' Jesus goes on to simply give his name and again describe himself as persecuted. His presence demands a response from Paul: to know Jesus not as an impersonal object to be eliminated, but as a grace-filled person to be followed.

Draw close to us, Lord Jesus, in the big questions of life.
Show us your way, your truth and your life.

TERRY HINKS

Faith proclaimed

'After that, King Agrippa, I was not disobedient to the heavenly vision, but declared first to those in Damascus, then in Jerusalem and throughout the countryside of Judea, and also to the Gentiles, that they should repent and turn to God and do deeds consistent with repentance. For this reason the Jews seized me in the temple and tried to kill me. To this day I have had help from God, and so I stand here, testifying to both small and great, saying nothing but what the prophets and Moses said would take place: that the Messiah must suffer, and that, by being the first to rise from the dead, he would proclaim light both to our people and to the Gentiles.'

The vision on the road leads on to the task of sharing the message, and soon Paul is reaching out into the surrounding area and moving beyond his own Jewish community to speak to Gentiles too. The message he proclaims has the same key elements of the gospel as are shared by the other preachers in Acts. Paul speaks of the need for God to help him in this work. He outlines the essence of the good news as: relying on the witness of the Hebrew scriptures to point people to the suffering Messiah, Jesus; proclaiming the one who, 'being the first to rise from the dead', brings hope to a hurting world; one who is light, not only to the Jewish people, but also to the Gentiles; and challenging all to repent, turn to God, and reflect that new beginning in changed lives.

This is a universal message, not limited to one part of society, the 'spiritual', 'religious' or 'intellectual'. While speaking to King Agrippa, Paul makes clear that his message is for 'both small and great'. There is no hierarchy of importance in the kingdom of God and the message of Jesus. In fact, it is good that he puts the word 'small' first, for it is a reminder of God's deep concern for the 'little ones'. As Jesus said and demonstrated, 'Not one [sparrow] will fall to the ground unperceived by your Father' (Matthew 10:29).

Who are the 'small ones' for you today?
How can the gospel speak to them?

TERRY HINKS

Speaking freely

But Paul said, 'I am not out of my mind, most excellent Festus, but I am speaking the sober truth. Indeed the king knows about these things, and to him I speak freely; for I am certain that none of these things has escaped his notice, for this was not done in a corner. King Agrippa, do you believe the prophets? I know that you believe.' Agrippa said to Paul, 'Are you so quickly persuading me to become a Christian?' Paul replied, 'Whether quickly or not, I pray to God that not only you but also all who are listening to me today might become such as I am – except for these chains.'

There are times in Acts when Luke's picture of Paul seems at odds with the Paul portrayed by his own writing. To me this passage does not seem to be such a place, for Paul's words feel very much in character. Accused by Festus of crazy talk, Paul replies with conviction and courage. Accused by Agrippa of trying to make him a Christian, Paul replies with equal quick-wittedness.

So here we see Paul's courage as he refuses to be intimidated by his questioners. We see his intellectual rigour as he relates his faith to the prophets of the past and the reality of the present. We see his deep desire for others to experience the grace and love of God as he has met in Jesus and the Spirit's fruit. His longing for his hearers to 'become such as I am' is not about his own self-importance, but of what God has done for and in him. As he told the Philippian Christians, 'Keep on doing the things that you have learned and received and heard and seen in me, and the God of peace will be with you' (Philippians 4:9). We then see his sense of drama, irony and humour, as he adds the footnote 'except these chains'.

Here are qualities to learn and hold on to today, as we share God's unchained word in our complex and confusing 21st–century world: courage in our witness, rigour in our thinking, love for others in our sharing and humour and hope in our speaking.

'But the word of God is not chained' (2 Timothy 2:9b).

TERRY HINKS

The care of friends

When it was decided that we were to sail for Italy, they transferred Paul and some other prisoners to a centurion of the Augustan Cohort, named Julius. Embarking on a ship of Adramyttium that was about to set sail to the ports along the coast of Asia, we put to sea, accompanied by Aristarchus, a Macedonian from Thessalonica. The next day we put in at Sidon; and Julius treated Paul kindly, and allowed him to go to his friends to be cared for.

Luke is a master storyteller, and at this point he shifts from third person to first person, making his narrative all the more direct and personal. It draws us closer to the confused events of sailing from one port to another, hugging the coast to avoid the worst of the winds and storms. Characters in the events are named, perhaps because the church knows and remembers these people with affection. Julius, the centurion, in charge of the prisoners and responsible for taking them to Rome, is described as treating Paul kindly, an echo of other centurions who played their part in the story of Jesus. A Macedonian, Aristarchus, is named too, a fellow Christian mentioned earlier in the story of Acts, in the letter to the Colossians and in the letter to Philemon, where Paul describes him as a fellow worker who joins him in sending greetings. Whether known to Paul or not, the unnamed friends at Sidon offered him their friendship and care. Paul cannot have undergone the months of imprisonment and the journeys without some suffering, physically and mentally, and to be cared for in this way must have been a moment of huge relief and encouragement.

In our Christian lives we need to be able 'to go to friends to be cared for', to have those spaces where in the company of a loyal friend we can recover ourselves, refresh our hearts and be encouraged for the journey ahead. Loneliness has reached epidemic levels in the west, and so let us pray that, like Julius, we may treat people kindly and, like Aristarchus, we would be a friend who is there for another person in their hardest times.

Who needs you to be a friend to them today?
How can you show them that you care?

TERRY HINKS

Hope abandoned

We were being pounded by the storm so violently that on the next day they began to throw the cargo overboard, and on the third day with their own hands they threw the ship's tackle overboard. When neither sun nor stars appeared for many days, and no small tempest raged, all hope of our being saved was at last abandoned.

The ship on which Paul is being taken to Rome is caught in a terrifying storm. Nature is unleashed in all its immense power, and the sailors of the fragile craft wrestle to keep it from sinking. The storm obscures the sun and stars, making navigation impossible. Caught up in the story, we can sense the darkness and despair as we reach the point where Luke says, 'All hope of our being saved was abandoned.'

Storms of this magnitude remind us that the planet is not here to do our bidding. It has a life of its own and a power that we cannot control. We may affect the climate by our carbon emissions and global warming, but the result is chaotic rather than controllable. Our increasing knowledge and understanding should lead not to arrogance and exploitation, but a proper sense of awe, humility and care.

That sense of helplessness can also lead at times to a feeling of despair. In the past few years, the Covid-19 pandemic and its economic and social impact, together with the environmental crisis, have led many to feel hopeless and helpless. The world can seem a very dark place.

Luke invites us to enter that place in the eye of the storm, in empathy and lament; to experience, even if only for a moment, what it feels to have all hope drain away. It is a real place for many people across the world. We have seen it vividly in the stories of refugees struggling to get across uncertain waters in the flimsiest boats. And perhaps we have experienced it in our own lives, in the face of health problems or relationship breakdown.

It is into this dark and threatening space that Paul will share a message of hope, assuring everyone that God has not abandoned them.

Remember today those travelling across the sea,
in whatever craft that may be.

TERRY HINKS

Food shared

Just before daybreak, Paul urged all of them to take some food, saying, 'Today is the fourteenth day that you have been in suspense and remaining without food, having eaten nothing. Therefore I urge you to take some food, for it will help you survive; for none of you will lose a hair from your heads.' After he had said this, he took bread; and giving thanks to God in the presence of all, he broke it and began to eat. Then all of them were encouraged and took food for themselves.

Food is the stuff of life: enjoyed in simple home cooking and elaborate feasts, eaten at family celebrations and shared symbolically in many religions. Today we are even more conscious of what we eat: its origins (and food miles), its health benefits (or problems), its cost and availability. 'Food insecurity' has entered our vocabularies to describe those who struggle to feed themselves or their families, relying increasingly on the help of food banks.

At its most basic, food is what nourishes and enables us to function properly. Paul recognises this as he looks at those on board the battered ship, so caught up with keeping the boat afloat that they had not eaten for days. He is both practical and sensitive to their needs when he tells them to eat; at this point they need food simply to survive the shipwreck to come.

Still, they are slow to respond, so Paul himself begins to eat, giving thanks to God as he breaks bread in their presence. Here is a glorious sacred moment. This is not an upper room, but a wet and storm-tossed boat, yet Christ is truly present in the breaking of bread. Not many on board would recognise this, but the impact was real. They took courage and took food.

Here is a truly eucharistic action, connecting the ordinary bread needed to survive with the living bread that speaks of Christ's saving work for the whole world. It is no accident that food banks have often involved local churches, with Christians wanting to respond to the physical needs of the people of their community alongside their spiritual ones.

Remember those who will not have a proper meal today
and the work of your local food bank.

TERRY HINKS

All safe

But striking a reef, they ran the ship aground; the bow stuck and remained immovable, but the stern was being broken up by the force of the waves. The soldiers' plan was to kill the prisoners, so that none might swim away and escape; but the centurion, wishing to save Paul, kept them from carrying out their plan. He ordered those who could swim to jump overboard first and make for the land, and the rest to follow, some on planks and others on pieces of the ship. And so it was that all were brought safely to land.

We watch with fascination and dread reports of rescue missions following earthquakes, shipwrecks, fires or accidents. An injured caver brought to the surface after days underground; miners rescued after being trapped deep below the surface; desperate people in a flimsy inflatable boat lifted to safety; a child brought out safely from a burning building. The joy and relief of these successful rescue missions are palpable. Today's emergency and rescue services have amazing equipment to aid their work, but they still rely on the dedication, courage and expertise of each member of the team, risking all for the good of others.

There was no rescue team to help when the ship ran aground with Paul and all the other prisoners, sailors and soldiers. With the ship breaking up, all were staring death in the face and that was doubly true for the prisoners under threat of death in case they escaped. Yet again a quick-thinking centurion plays his part, preventing the soldiers killing the prisoners and ordering everyone off the boat. By one means or another, amid all the chaos and currents, every person is able to get to land.

What a glorious moment that must have been when it was known that all were safe. 'All' is a small but very powerful word. None are excluded, none are left out. It echoes God's love for all, embracing not only all humanity but the whole of the natural world. Here is a glimpse of God's saving work, bringing bedraggled humanity to safety in Christ and renewing the face of the earth.

Pray for all who serve in emergency and rescue services in their work today.

TERRY HINKS

Around a fire

After we had reached safety, we then learned that the island was called Malta. The natives showed us unusual kindness. Since it had begun to rain and was cold, they kindled a fire and welcomed all of us round it… They bestowed many honours on us, and when we were about to sail, they put on board all the provisions we needed.

The kindness of strangers is a wonderful thing. Recovering from the trauma of the storm and shipwreck, soaking wet and cold, Paul and the others are invited by the local Maltese people to gather round a fire to warm themselves. This is common humanity at work, people working together for each other's good, irrespective of background or race.

Paul gathers brushwood to add to the fire and in due course survives a snake bite, causing the local people to wonder if a god is in their midst. Paul is no god, but his humanity is touched by God's Spirit, empowering him to bring help and healing to the people.

We know of Paul the great teacher, but there is no mention in this story of the message being shared verbally. Naturally there would have been much talk around the campfire, and Paul no doubt spoke of the good news of Jesus, but it is not mentioned here. Instead, Luke focuses on caring actions, in the hospitality of the local people and then Paul's ministry of prayer and healing among them. The hands that he had warmed beside the fire were used in the following days to pray for wholeness and health for those burdened by illness. In turn Paul and his companions are honoured and eventually sent on their way on another ship. Having lost everything in the shipwreck, they are given all the provisions they need for the journey ahead.

The strong Maltese church today traces its roots back to this event: a moment when mutual care and compassion sowed the seeds of faith. There is a human warmth here that echoes the warmth of the fire and reflects the warmth of God's love. In our own times, can we transcend all that divides people and come together in a place of warmth and safety?

Pray for those in need of warmth and shelter today.

TERRY HINKS

Take courage

Three months later we set sail on a ship that had wintered at the island, an Alexandrian ship with the Twin Brothers as its figurehead. We put in at Syracuse… Rhegium… and… Puteoli. There we found believers and were invited to stay with them for seven days. And so we came to Rome. The believers from there, when they heard of us, came as far as the Forum of Appius and Three Taverns to meet us. On seeing them, Paul thanked God and took courage.

The long and challenging journey is over. Paul's arrival at Rome is very significant, but he is by no means the first Christian in the city. Christian communities had been growing across the city and they come out to meet Paul and his companions. Paul had already written to the church in Rome, a treatise presenting his theology to a church he hoped to visit. He had met Christian tradespeople who lived there and had many different contacts with the church communities. Yet his hope to visit Rome was only now being fulfilled, though not as he might originally have planned.

Paul's journey from coast to city has the feel of a triumphant procession. His letter clearly had made a huge impact on the church in Rome, because the local Christians come out as far as the Forum of Appius, 40 miles from the city. Others meet him at Three Taverns, a little closer on the way, and no doubt accompany the party into the city.

This meeting with the Christians of Rome is a powerful moment. Just as his letters to the churches begin with thanksgiving, so here Paul begins by giving thanks to God. This motley group of people of different backgrounds, races and status is a sight to gladden the heart, giving him courage for whatever unknown challenges he will face in Rome. Here is the body of Christ at work, as Paul had described in his letter to them: 'So in Christ we, though many, form one body, and each member belongs to all the others' (Romans 12:5, NIV).

For those we meet along the way today, thanks be to God.
For those who encourage us on the way, thanks be to God.

TERRY HINKS

Paul preaches in Rome

After they had fixed a day to meet him, they came to him at his lodgings in great numbers. From morning until evening he explained the matter to them, testifying to the kingdom of God and trying to convince them about Jesus both from the law of Moses and from the prophets. Some were convinced by what he had said, while others refused to believe.

The local Jewish leaders are interested to hear more of Paul's message, having not heard any reports for or against him, so they fix a day to meet him. A large crowd gathers at Paul's quarters and for the whole day Paul speaks about Jesus and God's kingdom. The reaction is mixed and while some take the message to heart, many do not. Paul is saddened and quotes from the prophet Isaiah about the people's hearts becoming dull.

Was this the point when the church began to turn from being a Jewish movement that drew in Gentiles to being essentially a non-Jewish community? Rome is clearly symbolic of the gospel reaching the heart of the Gentile world, but faith is not something to force on others or deny to them. Some in the Roman Jewish community accepted Jesus as their Messiah. Others did not. This God-given freedom remains and is to be respected.

In the centuries since, horrific persecution has at times been inflicted on Jewish people by Christians, with scripture used and twisted to justify such horrors. In 1222, the Synod of Oxford (a council of the church in England – Catholic at the time) issued a series of edicts which included one forcing Jewish people to wear a badge, a horrific precursor of the Nazi's 'Jewish Star' badge. The 800th anniversary of that event in 2022 was an opportunity for the present-day church to express its repentance of past actions and prejudice and its solidarity with the Jewish community today, as it faces increasingly aggressive antisemitism.

While Christians and Jews disagree about whether Jesus is the promised Messiah, there is much that they hold in common, not least the Hebrew scriptures, the desire to seek God's kingdom of peace and justice and their shared love for God, the one and only creator and redeemer.

Pray for good relationships between Christians and Jews,
and between people of all faiths and none.

TERRY HINKS

135

Not the end

'Let it be known to you then that this salvation of God has been sent to the Gentiles; they will listen.' He lived there for two whole years at his own expense and welcomed all who came to him, proclaiming the kingdom of God and teaching about the Lord Jesus Christ with all boldness and without hindrance.

Luke ended his first book with Jesus telling the disciples that they will be his witnesses, beginning in Jerusalem and reaching out to all nations, and promising that they will receive the Holy Spirit to empower them for this task (Luke 24:44–49). He ends his second book with Paul doing just that at the heart of the Roman empire, reaching out beyond his own Jewish community to the Gentiles. There is a sense of the Holy Spirit at work, opening new doors and giving boldness to Paul's message.

Tradition has it that Paul died a martyr's death, executed as part of Emperor Nero's persecution of Christians. There are hints in Acts that this is to be Paul's fate, but Luke ends his story with Paul alive and active. He may be under house arrest, with a guard on duty, but that doesn't prevent people coming to see him and hear his message. He welcomes all.

As we conclude our reflections on the end of the book of Acts, it is good to refocus our attention on the kingdom of God and the teaching of Jesus. The kingdom of God is full of life, joy and peace, in contrast to the Roman empire (and the empires which have followed) with its false peace. The crucified and risen Jesus is Lord and Saviour, in contrast to the twisted, violent and fading power of the emperor (and all tyrants who have come since). We have followed Paul on a tortuous journey to Rome, the centre of political power, but he would not have wanted that power to distract us from the heart of the faith: the love of God in Christ Jesus, stronger than life, stronger than death. Thank God for Paul's vibrant and faithful teaching of that good news.

God of abundant life, give us boldness this day to seek your kingdom and share the love of Christ.

TERRY HINKS

Become a Friend of BRF
and give regularly to support our ministry

We help people of all ages to grow in faith

We encourage and support individual Christians and churches as they serve and resource the changing spiritual needs of communities today.

Through **Anna Chaplaincy** we're enabling churches to provide spiritual care to older people

Through **Living Faith** we're nurturing faith and resourcing life long discipleship

Through **Messy Church** we're helping churches to reach out to families

Through **Parenting for Faith** we're supporting parents as they raise their children in the Christian faith

Our ministry is only possible because of the generous support of individuals, churches, trusts and gifts in wills.

As we look to the future and make plans, **regular donations make a huge difference** in ensuring we can both start and finish projects well.

By becoming a Friend of BRF and giving regularly to our ministry you are partnering with us in the gospel and helping change lives.

How your gift makes a difference

£2 a month — Helps us to give away **Living Faith** resources via food banks and chaplaincy services

£10 a month — Helps us to support parents and churches running the **Parenting for Faith** course

£5 a month — Helps us to support **Messy Church** volunteers and grow the wider network

£20 a month — Helps us to develop the reach of **Anna Chaplaincy** and improve spiritual care for older people

How to become a Friend of BRF

Online – set up a Direct Debit donation at brf.org.uk/donate or find out how to set up a Standing Order at brf.org.uk/friends

By post – complete and return the tear-off form opposite to 'Freepost BRF' (*no other address or stamp is needed*)

If you have any questions, or if you want to change your regular donation or stop giving in the future, do get in touch.

Contact the fundraising team

Email: giving@brf.org.uk
Tel: 01235 462305
Post: Fundraising team, BRF, 15 The Chambers, Vineyard, Abingdon OX14 3FE

Registered with **FUNDRAISING REGULATOR**

Bible Reading Fellowship (BRF) is a charity (233280) and company limited by guarantee (301324), registered in England and Wales

SHARING OUR VISION – MAKING A GIFT

I would like to make a donation to support BRF.
Please use my gift for:

☐ Where the need is greatest ☐ Anna Chaplaincy ☐ Living Faith

☐ Messy Church ☐ Parenting for Faith

Title	First name/initials	Surname
Address		
		Postcode
Email		
Telephone		
Signature		Date

Our ministry is only possible because of the generous support of individuals, churches, trusts and gifts in wills.

Please treat as Gift Aid donations all qualifying gifts of money made

giftaid it

☐ today, ☐ in the past four years, ☐ and in the future.

I am a UK taxpayer and understand that if I pay less Income Tax and/or Capital Gains Tax in the current tax year than the amount of Gift Aid claimed on all my donations, it is my responsibility to pay any difference.

☐ My donation does not qualify for Gift Aid.

Please notify BRF if you want to cancel this Gift Aid declaration, change your name or home address, or no longer pay sufficient tax on your income and/or capital gains.

You can also give online at **brf.org.uk/donate**, which reduces our administration costs, making your donation go further.

Please complete other side of form ➡

SHARING OUR VISION – MAKING A GIFT

Please accept my gift of:

☐ £2 ☐ £5 ☐ £10 ☐ £20 Other £ [   ]

by (*delete as appropriate*):

☐ Cheque/Charity Voucher payable to 'BRF'

☐ MasterCard/Visa/Debit card/Charity card

Name on card

Card no. [ ][ ][ ][ ] [ ][ ][ ][ ] [ ][ ][ ][ ] [ ][ ][ ][ ]

Expires end [M][M] [Y][Y] Security code* [ ][ ][ ] *Last 3 digits on the reverse of the card

Signature	Date

☐ I would like to leave a gift to BRF in my will.
   Please send me further information.

☐ I'd like to find out about giving a regular gift to BRF.

For help or advice regarding making a gift, please contact our fundraising team +44 (0)1865 462305

Your privacy

We will use your personal data to process this transaction. From time to time we may send you information about the work of BRF that we think may be of interest to you. Our privacy policy is available at **brf.org.uk/privacy**. Please contact us if you wish to discuss your mailing preferences.

Registered with

FUNDRAISING **REGULATOR**

◄ Please complete other side of form

Please return this form to 'Freepost BRF'
No other address information or stamp is needed

Bible Reading Fellowship is a charity (233280) and company limited by guarantee (301324), registered in England and Wales

Overleaf… Reading *New Daylight* in a group | Author profile | Recommended reading | Order and subscription forms

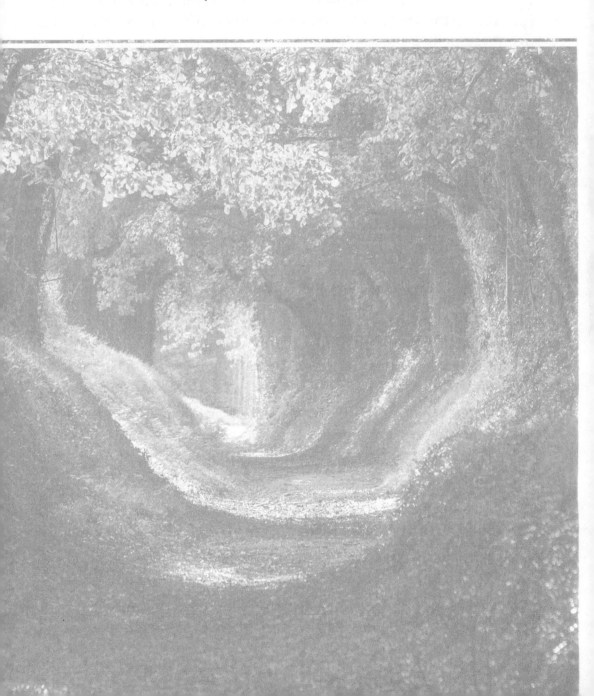

Reading *New Daylight* in a group

GORDON GILES

In the Rule of Benedict, which formed the spiritual foundations of the daily prayer life of so many ecclesiastical foundations, daily reading was a key aspect of the community life of work and prayer. The distinct disciplines of reading scripture alone and reading together were both significant in the spiritual and moral formation of the monks of all ranks. With these daily Bible reading notes, we offer scripture and reflective material for personal reading. Yet discussion or shared reflection on the passages chosen and the comments made can also be rewarding, so we also offer some open questions that may enable discussion in a Bible study or other group who gather to take further what is published here. The same questions may also aid personal devotion. Use them as you wish, and may God bless and inspire you on your journey as you read holy words and ponder them in your heart.

General discussion starters

These can be used for any study series within this issue. Remember there are no right or wrong answers – these questions are simply to enable a group to engage in conversation.

- What do you think is the main idea or theme of the author in this series? Did that come across strongly?

- Have any of the issues discussed touched on personal – or shared – specifics of your life?

- What evidence or stories do the authors draw on to illuminate, or be illuminated by the passages of scripture.

- Which do you prefer: scripture informing daily modern life, or modern life shining a new light on scripture?

- Does the author 'call you to action' in a realistic and achievable way? Do you think their ideas will work in the secular world?

- Have any specific passages struck you personally? If so, how and why? Is God speaking to you through scripture and reflection?

- Was anything completely new to you? Were there any 'eureka' or jaw-dropping moments? If so, what difference will that make?

Questions for specific series

The Word made flesh: John 1—2 (Amy Boucher Pye)

- As you begin the new year with John's gospel, what are your hopes and fears for yourself, for your community and for the world?
- What physical and spiritual images do the words 'dwelling' and 'remain' conjure up for you? What does it mean to dwell in God and for God to dwell in us?
- What does it mean to be a follower of Jesus in the 21st century?
- The opening of John's gospel contains signs and miracles. Which is more important, the miraculous event or the meaning it carries?

David (David Walker)

- If you have a biblical name, how do you feel about that? If you do not, which biblical name would you choose for yourself and why? Does your name affect who you turn out to be?
- David had an eventful life, with spiritual lows and highs. Can you relate to him, or are his life and times too remote for us now?
- Think about the women involved in David's story. What impact does he have on their lives? How does that make you feel about them and about him?
- Was David a good man? Discuss...

Spring (Liz Hoare)

- Are you affected by the seasons? How do you feel about the advent of spring? Lent means 'spring' – how are the two connected?
- How can the image of a tree be helpful in contemplating the life of faith? Where or what are your roots, your branches, your blossoms, your fruit and your seeds?
- In your community or church, where are the green shoots of hope pushing through the darkness, and what can you do to encourage and nurture this?
- What invitations to grow, opportunities to blossom or other possibilities is Lent offering you this year?

Paul's journey to Rome: Acts 25—29 (Terry Hinks)

- Imagine yourself in Paul's situation at the end of Acts, being arrested, put on trial, falsely accused, threatened with execution and ending up shipwrecked. How does that make you feel?

- Apart from celebrating Holy Communion in church, how can other meals or contexts in which food is given or shared take on dimensions of thanksgiving, remembrance, fellowship and generosity under God?

- Do you like to travel? Reflect on some of the journeys you have made and compare them with Paul's arduous trips around Asia Minor. Would you like to see the places he saw? Look them up on a map or check them out on the internet. Does this make his adventures seem more real to you?

- The end of Acts is the last we hear of Paul's life, mission, ministry and journeying. How do you feel about his significant contribution to the early life and ministry of Christ's church? Could anyone else have done it better, or even at all? If so, how? If not, why not?

Meet the author: Archbishop Andy John

Tell us about your Christian journey.
My Christian journey begins with a typical chapel upbringing in my home town in Wales. I found any excuse not to go to church and avoided confirmation at the age of 14. But an encounter with some Christians of my age some four years later transformed my understanding of what it meant to be a Christian. I discovered, to my initial shock and then delight, that following Jesus was the best of all choices, and he has been the focus of my life ever since. Archbishops have some responsibility in the life of the church, but nothing touches the importance of being found in and living for Jesus.

How long have you been writing for *New Daylight*?
I am delighted to be associated with BRF and have been writing for them for seven years. As a young Christian I was taught the value of Bible and prayer, of 'quiet time' with God. To now provide material that enables others to draw close to God is a privilege. Whenever I write for BRF, my prayer is that God's written word will become a living word in the lives of those who read it and will enable them to become better disciples of Christ.

What is the chief joy of Christian ministry?
The joy of ministry for me, whether as an archbishop or parish priest, is to see people meeting with God in a transforming way, whether that is something small or something life-changing. God is full of endless surprises. God is always ahead of us and offers boundless grace for us to discover.

And of mission?
The church doesn't always get the credit it deserves for the work it does in our communities. We are at the heart of national life, serving others in specific and measurable ways. In the words of Jesus, being light and salt. I would love the church to cherish and enjoy the task of blessing the world a little more. Mission is in our DNA; we were made for this and being liberated into this kind of service would be wonderful.

Does the Welsh Christian heritage inspire you?
Wales is a land full of stories and saints who came and evangelised the land. These were the pioneers, risk-takers and missionaries who broke new ground. I love their adventurous spirit and pray for more of the same here and now.

145

Recommended reading

Lent is traditionally a time of repentance, fasting and prayer as we prepare to celebrate our salvation at Easter. Through daily readings and reflections from Ash Wednesday to Easter Day, Amy Scott Robinson explores different biblical images of repentance, sin, forgiveness and grace, bringing them together in Holy Week as a lens through which to view Christ's work of reconciliation on the cross.

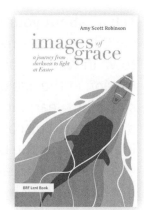

The following extract is taken from Monday's reflection in week two, on images of forgiveness.

> The Lord is merciful and gracious,
>   slow to anger and abounding in steadfast love.
> He will not always accuse,
>   nor will he keep his anger forever.
> He does not deal with us according to our sins,
>   nor repay us according to our iniquities.
> For as the heavens are high above the earth,
>   so great is his steadfast love toward those who fear him;
> as far as the east is from the west,
>   so far he removes our transgressions from us.
>
> PSALM 103:8–12

We really do have a problem with rubbish on our planet. In 2021, the world contained about 8.3 billion tons of plastic – of which about 6.3 billion tons was rubbish. That number can only increase, as plastic waste doesn't biodegrade and often releases toxic gases as it breaks down into smaller and smaller pieces. A single plastic bottle will take about 450 years to break down completely, but the plastic still hasn't actually gone away – it just isn't bottle-shaped any more. It has become tiny plastic particles in the soil, in the ocean, in drinking water. Even when we manage to scoop plastic waste out of the rivers and oceans, we don't have anywhere safe to put it. Wouldn't it be wonderful if somebody could just reach down and take it all far, far away?

What is impossible with plastic is somehow possible with sin – a substance which is just as long-lasting, harmful and insidious to the soul as plastic is to the earth. In Psalm 103 – attributed, like Psalm 51, to David – the singer addresses his own soul, telling himself to bless the Lord who forgives, heals and redeems. He paints a picture of God's character as a compassionate father (verse 13), who is slow to anger and full of love.

In verse 10, David writes that God does not repay us according to our iniquities. In a psalm full of assurances of God's steadfast love and forgiveness, our sins and iniquities are still described as something for which we deserve some sort of payment, and as something attached to or belonging to us: our sins, our iniquities. Earlier in the psalm, David has praised God as one who works justice for the oppressed (verse 6). It is not enough for David to describe God as loving while acknowledging that sin exists; something has to be done about it for us to receive God's love.

In the next two verses, David describes two great distances: the distance between the heavens and the earth, and the distance between the east and the west.

In verse 11, he says that as high as the heavens are above the earth, so great is God's steadfast love towards those who fear him. Beautifully, in describing the enormous distance between earth and heaven, between people and God, David fills that distance with the steadfast love of God, so that we have a picture of God's love bridging the gap between heaven and earth.

Then, in verse 12, David describes the space between the east and the west as the distance that God removes our transgressions from us. As the vertical distance is filled by God's love, the horizontal distance is emptied of human wrongdoing.

These two verses, with their vertical and horizontal planes, form a shape in the imagination. Writing long before Christ, reflecting on God's grace, David describes forgiveness in the shape of a cross: God's love stretching from heaven to earth, sins removed from east to west.

At this point, David is not just describing individual sin, but the sins of a people; and we can read it as describing the sin of all humanity. Through the cross, we look forward to a time when it will all be removed. Not just the ways we have hurt others, but the ways they have hurt us, and the ways in which all people collectively have caused damage, and the reason for it all – all will be lifted away and we will not have to bear any of it any longer.

We really do have a problem with rubbish on this planet, and sadly, the plastic isn't going to be magically lifted away. The consequences of human sin, in this instance, are plain for all to see in the lasting damage we do to the earth. But what if we thought of sin itself as just as clinging,

147

damaging, toxic and indestructible – just as much of an eyesore, just as filthy as a landfill of plastic waste? Perhaps, then, we could appreciate the words of this psalm and be filled with gratitude at the prospect that God really does take it all away from us, as far as the east is from the west. We could feel the weight of it lifted off, and know that God sees us and treats us separately from our sin.

A question
If you had to draw 'sin', what would it look like? If you had to draw 'forgiveness', what would you draw?

A prayer
Gracious and compassionate Lord, thank you for your steadfast love. Thank you for taking all this horrible, heavy stuff so far away from me and for seeing me and loving me without it. I know that I can trust you as my compassionate father, who knows me so well that you will always be slow to anger and always full of love. Amen

To order a copy of this book, please use the order form on page 151 or visit **brfonline.org.uk**

On this journey from Ash Wednesday to Easter Day, you are invited to become a pilgrim with Brother Ramon. Each day there is the opportunity to stop and reflect on the gospel story, drawing insight from the experiences of those who were there during the events of the first Easter, finding inspiration and strength for the greater journey of our lives. Suffering and glory are intermingled in real human experience in this book, which is designed for personal and group use, for Christians of all traditions.

When They Crucified My Lord (BRF Centenary Classic)
Through Lenten sorrow to Easter joy
Brother Ramon SSF
978 1 80039 089 8 £14.99 HB
brfonline.org.uk

Using natural or manufactured objects, scenes, activities or places, Gordon Giles draws out spiritual insights to help us to reflect on what we have learnt and how we can walk with him as we venture out after many months of Covid-related restriction or absence. What is it like spiritually to stop wearing masks? What does a beach say to us after coronavirus? How has Zoom affected us during lockdown and how do we now relate to technology as a medium of fellowship?

At Home and Out and About
52 biblical contemplations on faith, hope and love
for a re-emerging world
Gordon Giles

978 1 80039 115 4 £9.99
brfonline.org.uk

To order

Online: brfonline.org.uk
Telephone: +44 (0)1865 319700
Mon–Fri 9.30–17.00

Delivery times within the UK are normally 15 working days. Prices are correct at the time of going to press but may change without prior notice.

Title	Price	Qty	Total
Images of Grace (BRF Lent book 2023)	£9.99		
At Home and Out and About	£9.99		
When They Crucified My Lord (BRF Centenary Classic)	£14.99		

POSTAGE AND PACKING CHARGES			
Order value	UK	Europe	Rest of world
Under £7.00	£2.00		
£7.00–£29.99	£3.00	Available on request	Available on request
£30.00 and over	FREE		

Total value of books	
Postage and packing	
Donation*	
Total for this order	

* Please complete and return the Gift Aid declaration on page 139.

Please complete in BLOCK CAPITALS

Title _____ First name/initials _____ Surname _____

Address _____

_____ Postcode _____

Acc. No. _____ Telephone _____

Email _____

Method of payment

☐ Cheque (made payable to BRF) ☐ MasterCard / Visa

Card no. ☐☐☐☐ ☐☐☐☐ ☐☐☐☐ ☐☐☐☐

Expires end [M][M] [Y][Y]   Security code ☐☐☐   Last 3 digits on the reverse of the card

We will use your personal data to process this order. From time to time we may send you information about the work of BRF. Please contact us if you wish to discuss your mailing preferences **brf.org.uk/privacy**

Please return this form to:

BRF, 15 The Chambers, Vineyard, Abingdon OX14 3FE | **enquiries@brf.org.uk**
For terms and cancellation information, please visit **brfonline.org.uk/terms**.

Bible Reading Fellowship (BRF) is a charity (233280) and company limited by guarantee (301324), registered in England and Wales

BRF needs you!

If you're one of our many thousands of regular *New Daylight* readers, you will know all about the impact that regular Bible reading has on your faith and the value of daily notes to guide, inform and inspire you.

Here are some recent comments from *New Daylight* readers:

'Thank you for all the many inspiring writings that help so much when things are tough.'

'Just right for me – I learned a lot!'

'We looked forward to each day's message as we pondered each passage and comment.'

If you have similarly positive things to say about *New Daylight*, would you be willing to share your experience with others? Perhaps you could give a short talk or write a brief article about why you find *New Daylight* so helpful. You could form a *New Daylight* reading group, perhaps supplying members with their first copy of the notes. Or you could pass on your back copies or give someone a gift subscription. However you do it, the important thing is to find creative ways to put a copy of *New Daylight* into someone else's hands.

It doesn't need to be complicated and we can help with group and bulk-buy discounts.

We can supply further information if you need it and and would love to hear about it if you do find ways to get *New Daylight* into new readers' hands.

For more information:

- Email **enquiries@brf.org.uk**
- Telephone BRF on +44 (0)1865 319700 Mon–Fri 9.30–17.00
- Write to us at BRF, 15 The Chambers, Vineyard, Abingdon OX14 3FE

Enabling all ages to grow in faith

At BRF, we long for people of all ages to grow in faith and understanding of the Bible. That's what all our work as a charity is about.

- BRF's **Living Faith** ministry looks to see our founder Leslie Mannering's vision – to help people 'get a move on' spiritually – fulfilled in the 21st century. Our wide range of resources promotes Bible reading and prayer, our events bring people together to share this journey, and our Holy Habits initiative helps congregations grow in whole-life discipleship.

- We also want to make it easier for local churches to engage effectively in ministry and mission – by helping them bring new families into a growing relationship with God through **Messy Church** or by supporting churches as they nurture the spiritual life of older people through **Anna Chaplaincy**.

- Our **Parenting for Faith** team coaches parents and others to raise God-connected children and teens, and enables churches to fully support them.

Do you share our vision?

Though a significant proportion of BRF's funding is generated through our charitable activities, we are dependent on the generous support of individuals, churches and charitable trusts.

If you share our vision, would you help us to enable even more people of all ages to grow in faith? Your prayers and financial support are vital for the work that we do. You could:

- support BRF's ministry with a regular donation
- support us with a one-off gift
- consider leaving a gift to BRF in your will
- encourage your church to support BRF as part of your church's giving to home mission – perhaps focusing on a specific ministry or project
- most important of all, support BRF with your prayers.

Donate at **brf.org.uk/donate** or use the form on pages 139–40.

Fruit that lasts

I no longer call you servants, because a servant does not know his master's business. Instead, I have called you friends, for everything that I learned from my Father I have made known to you. You did not choose me, but I chose you and appointed you so that you might go and bear fruit – fruit that will last – and so that whatever you ask in my name the Father will give you.

JOHN 15:15–16 (NIV)

In this verse Jesus is speaking to his disciples in the upper room, giving them a farewell and a sending out, words of comfort and empowerment to get them through the coming days. Here he makes it explicit, those gathered in the room are his friends. Their relationship has transcended that of master and servant through the sharing of knowledge. For a servant simply follows the orders of the master, while a friend with profound understanding can take initiative and carry ideas forward – and ultimately bear lasting fruit.

For over 100 years, BRF has been working to share the knowledge of the gospel with as many people of all ages as possible, whether through our Bible reading notes, like those you are now holding, or the wider work of our ministries – Anna Chaplaincy, Living Faith, Messy Church and Parenting for Faith. It is our goal not only to share the Bible but also to give people the tools for building a deeper understanding of and a closer friendship with God, which will then bear fruit in their own lives and in their communities.

Our work is made possible through kind donations from individuals, charitable trusts and gifts in wills. If you would like to support BRF's work you can become a Friend of BRF by making a monthly gift of £2 a month or more – we thank you for your friendship.

Find out more at **brf.org.uk/donate**.

Judith Moore
Fundraising development officer

> Give. Pray. Get involved.
> **brf.org.uk**

Please note our new subscription rates, current until 30 April 2024:

Individual subscriptions
covering 3 issues for under 5 copies, payable in advance
(including postage & packing):

	UK	Europe	Rest of world
New Daylight	£19.05	£26.55	£30.45
New Daylight 3-year subscription (9 issues) (not available for Deluxe)	£54.45	N/A	N/A
New Daylight Deluxe per set of 3 issues p.a.	£24.15	£33.00	£39.00

Group subscriptions
covering 3 issues for 5 copies or more, sent to one UK address (post free):

New Daylight	£14.85 per set of 3 issues p.a.
New Daylight Deluxe	£18.75 per set of 3 issues p.a.

Please note that the annual billing period for group subscriptions runs from 1 May to 30 April.

Overseas group subscription rates
Available on request. Please email **enquiries@brf.org.uk**.

Copies may also be obtained from Christian bookshops:

New Daylight	£4.95 per copy
New Daylight Deluxe	£6.25 per copy

All our Bible reading notes can be ordered online by visiting **brfonline.org.uk/subscriptions**

New Daylight is also available as an app for Android, iPhone and iPad **brfonline.org.uk/apps**

NEW DAYLIGHT INDIVIDUAL SUBSCRIPTION FORM

All our Bible reading notes can be ordered online by visiting
brfonline.org.uk/subscriptions

Title _____ First name/initials _____ Surname _____

Address _____

_____ Postcode _____

Telephone _____ Email _____

Please send *New Daylight* beginning with the May 2023 / September 2023 / January 2024 issue (*delete as appropriate*):

(*please tick box*)	UK	Europe	Rest of world
New Daylight 1-year subscription	☐ £19.05	☐ £26.55	☐ £30.45
New Daylight 3-year subscription	☐ £54.45	N/A	N/A
New Daylight Deluxe	☐ £24.15	☐ £33.00	☐ £39.00

Optional donation to support the work of BRF £ _____

Total enclosed £ _____ (cheques should be made payable to 'BRF')

Please complete and return the Gift Aid declaration on page 139 to make your donation even more valuable to us.

Please charge my MasterCard / Visa with £ _____

Card no. ☐☐☐☐ ☐☐☐☐ ☐☐☐☐ ☐☐☐☐

Expires end ☐☐ ☐☐   Security code ☐☐☐   Last 3 digits on the reverse of the card

To set up a Direct Debit, please complete the Direct Debit instruction on page 159.

We will use your personal data to process this order. From time to time we may send you information about the work of BRF. Please contact us if you wish to discuss your mailing preferences **brf.org.uk/privacy**

Please return this form with the appropriate payment to:
BRF, 15 The Chambers, Vineyard, Abingdon OX14 3FE
For terms and cancellation information, please visit **brfonline.org.uk/terms**.

Bible Reading Fellowship is a charity (233280) and company limited by guarantee (301324), registered in England and Wales

ND0123

NEW DAYLIGHT GIFT SUBSCRIPTION FORM

☐ I would like to give a gift subscription (please provide both names and addresses):

Title _____ First name/initials _____ Surname _____

Address _____

_____ Postcode _____

Telephone _____ Email _____

Gift subscription name _____

Gift subscription address _____

_____ Postcode _____

Gift message (20 words max. or include your own gift card):

_____

_____

Please send *New Daylight* beginning with the May 2023 / September 2023 / January 2024 issue (*delete as appropriate*):

(*please tick box*)	UK	Europe	Rest of world
New Daylight 1-year subscription	☐ £19.05	☐ £26.55	☐ £30.45
New Daylight 3-year subscription	☐ £54.45	N/A	N/A
New Daylight Deluxe	☐ £24.15	☐ £33.00	☐ £39.00

Optional donation to support the work of BRF £ _____

Total enclosed £ _____ (cheques should be made payable to 'BRF')

Please complete and return the Gift Aid declaration on page 139 to make your donation even more valuable to us.

Please charge my MasterCard / Visa with £ _____

Card no. ☐☐☐☐ ☐☐☐☐ ☐☐☐☐ ☐☐☐☐

Expires end ☐☐☐☐ Security code ☐☐ Last 3 digits on the reverse of the card

To set up a Direct Debit, please complete the Direct Debit instruction on page 159.

We will use your personal data to process this order. From time to time we may send you information about the work of BRF. Please contact us if you wish to discuss your mailing preferences **brf.org.uk/privacy**

Please return this form with the appropriate payment to:

BRF, 15 The Chambers, Vineyard, Abingdon OX14 3FE

For terms and cancellation information, please visit **brfonline.org.uk/terms**.

Bible Reading Fellowship is a charity (233280) and company limited by guarantee (301324), registered in England and Wales

You can pay for your annual subscription to our Bible reading notes using Direct Debit. You need only give your bank details once, and the payment is made automatically every year until you cancel it. If you would like to pay by Direct Debit, please use the form opposite, entering your BRF account number under 'Reference number'.

You are fully covered by the Direct Debit Guarantee:

The Direct Debit Guarantee

- This Guarantee is offered by all banks and building societies that accept instructions to pay Direct Debits.

- If there are any changes to the amount, date or frequency of your Direct Debit, Bible Reading Fellowship will notify you 10 working days in advance of your account being debited or as otherwise agreed. If you request Bible Reading Fellowship to collect a payment, confirmation of the amount and date will be given to you at the time of the request.

- If an error is made in the payment of your Direct Debit, by Bible Reading Fellowship or your bank or building society, you are entitled to a full and immediate refund of the amount paid from your bank or building society.

- If you receive a refund you are not entitled to, you must pay it back when Bible Reading Fellowship asks you to.

- You can cancel a Direct Debit at any time by simply contacting your bank or building society. Written confirmation may be required. Please also notify us.

Instruction to your bank or building society to pay by Direct Debit

Please fill in the whole form using a ballpoint pen and return with order form to:
BRF, 15 The Chambers, Vineyard, Abingdon OX14 3FE

Service User Number: | 5 | 5 | 8 | 2 | 2 | 9 |

Name and full postal address of your bank or building society

To: The Manager

Bank/Building Society

Address

Postcode

Name(s) of account holder(s)

Branch sort code

Bank/Building Society account number

Reference number

Instruction to your Bank/Building Society
Please pay Bible Reading Fellowship Direct Debits from the account detailed in this instruction, subject to the safeguards assured by the Direct Debit Guarantee. I understand that this instruction may remain with Bible Reading Fellowship and, if so, details will be passed electronically to my bank/building society.

Signature(s)

Banks and Building Societies may not accept Direct Debit instructions for some types of account.

Enabling all ages to grow in faith

Anna Chaplaincy

Living Faith

Messy Church

Parenting for Faith

BRF is a Christian charity that resources individuals and churches. Our vision is to enable people of all ages to grow in faith and understanding of the Bible and to see more people equipped to exercise their gifts in leadership and ministry.

To find out more about our work, visit
brf.org.uk